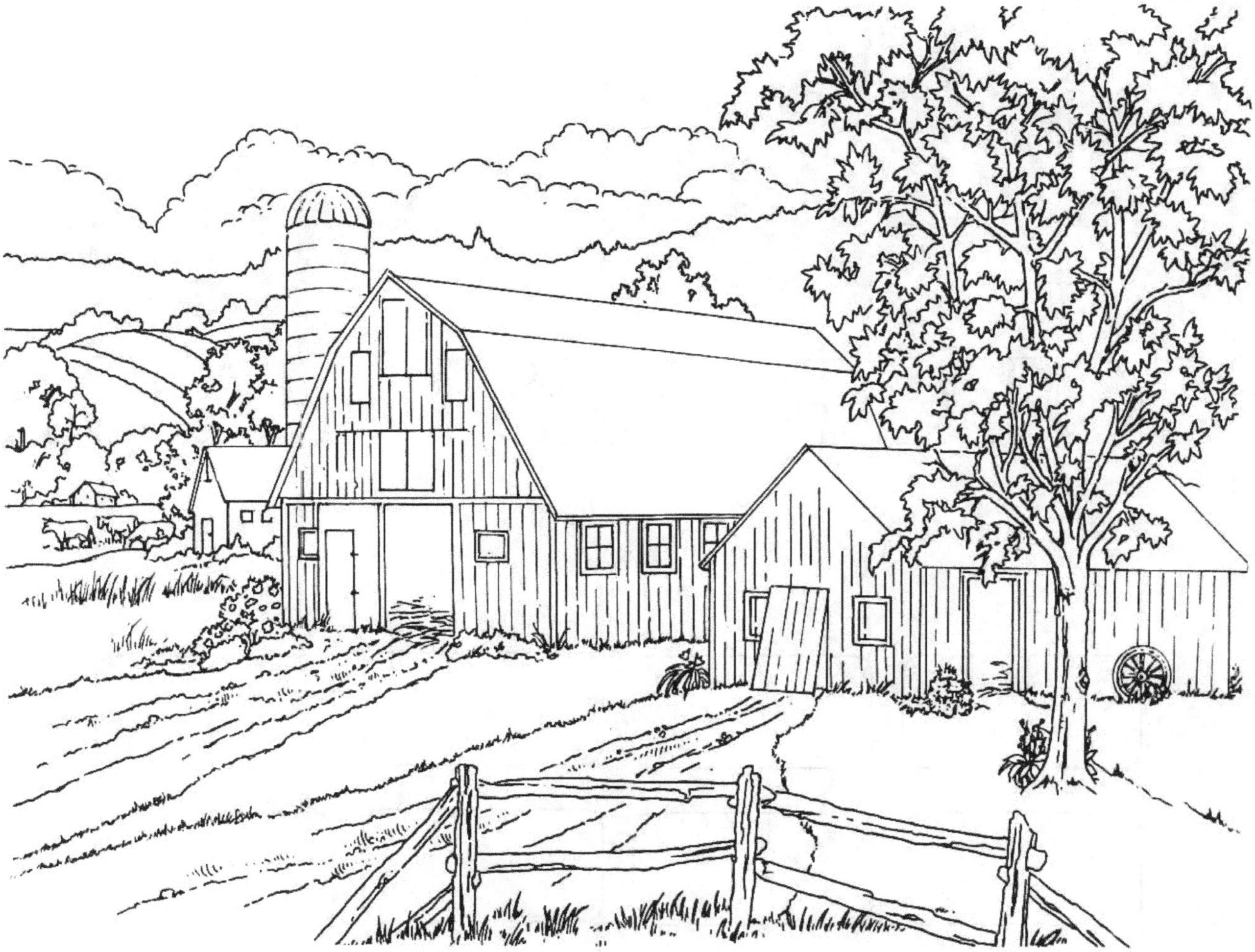

This Book Belongs To

COLOR TEST PAGE

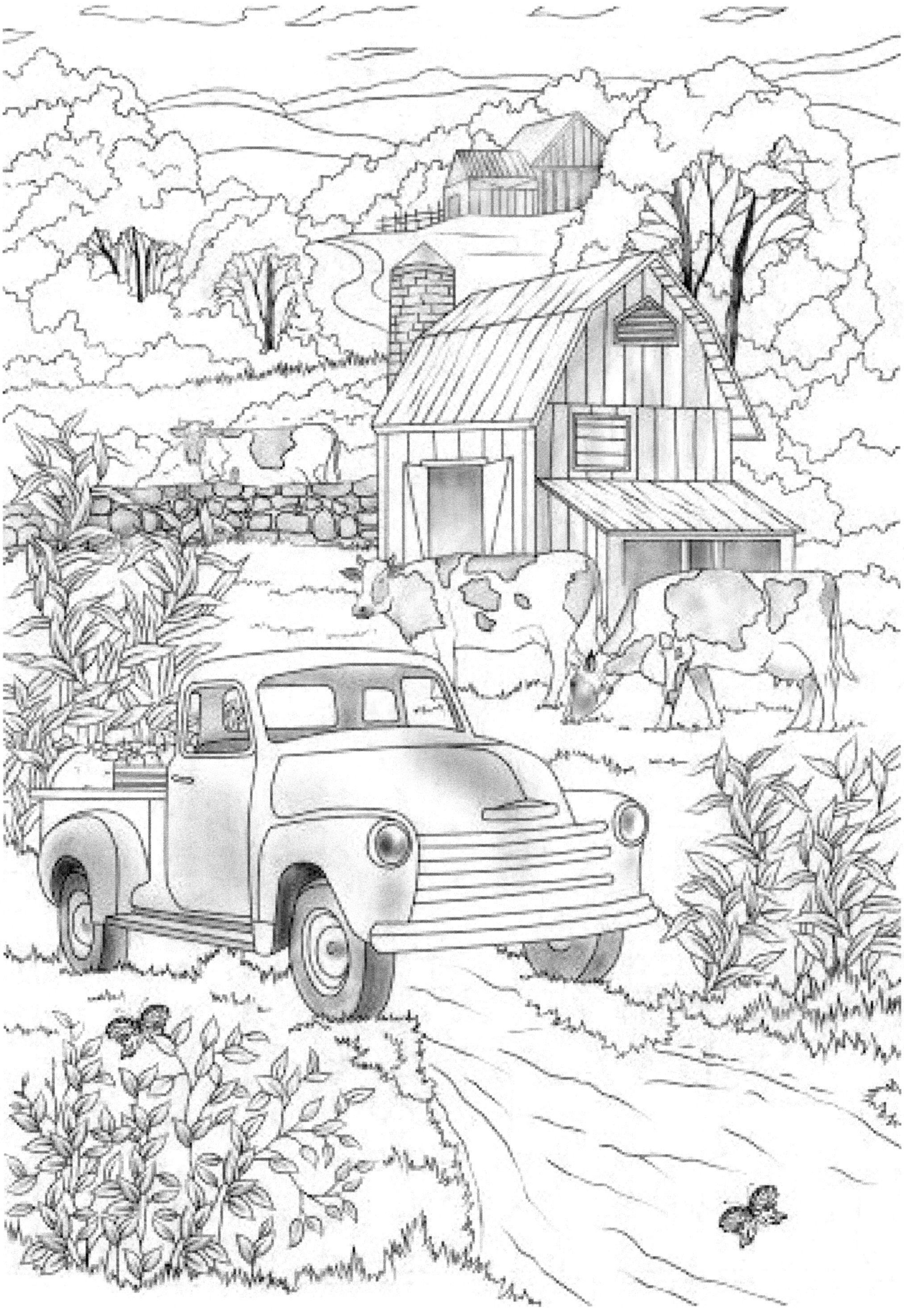

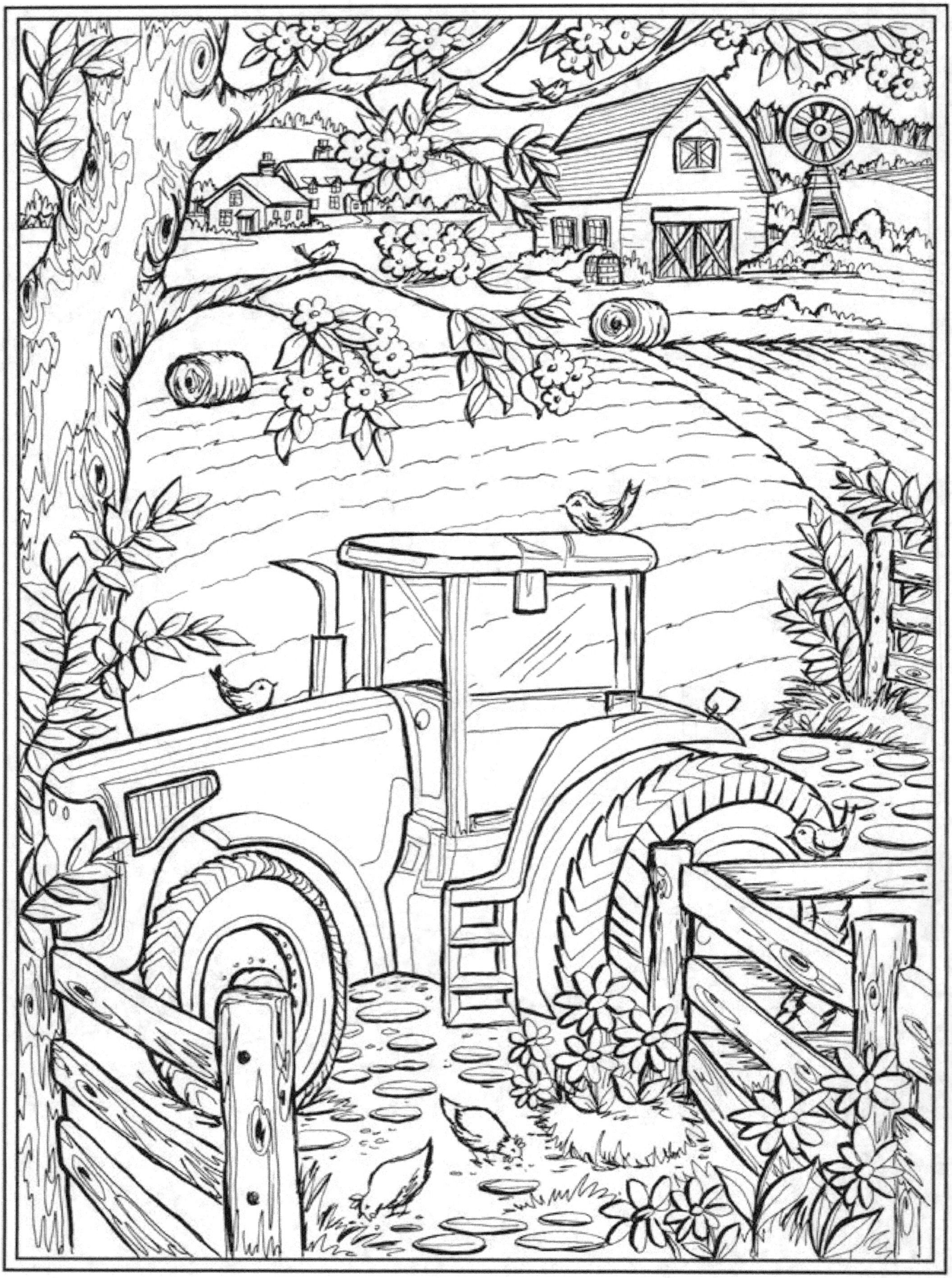

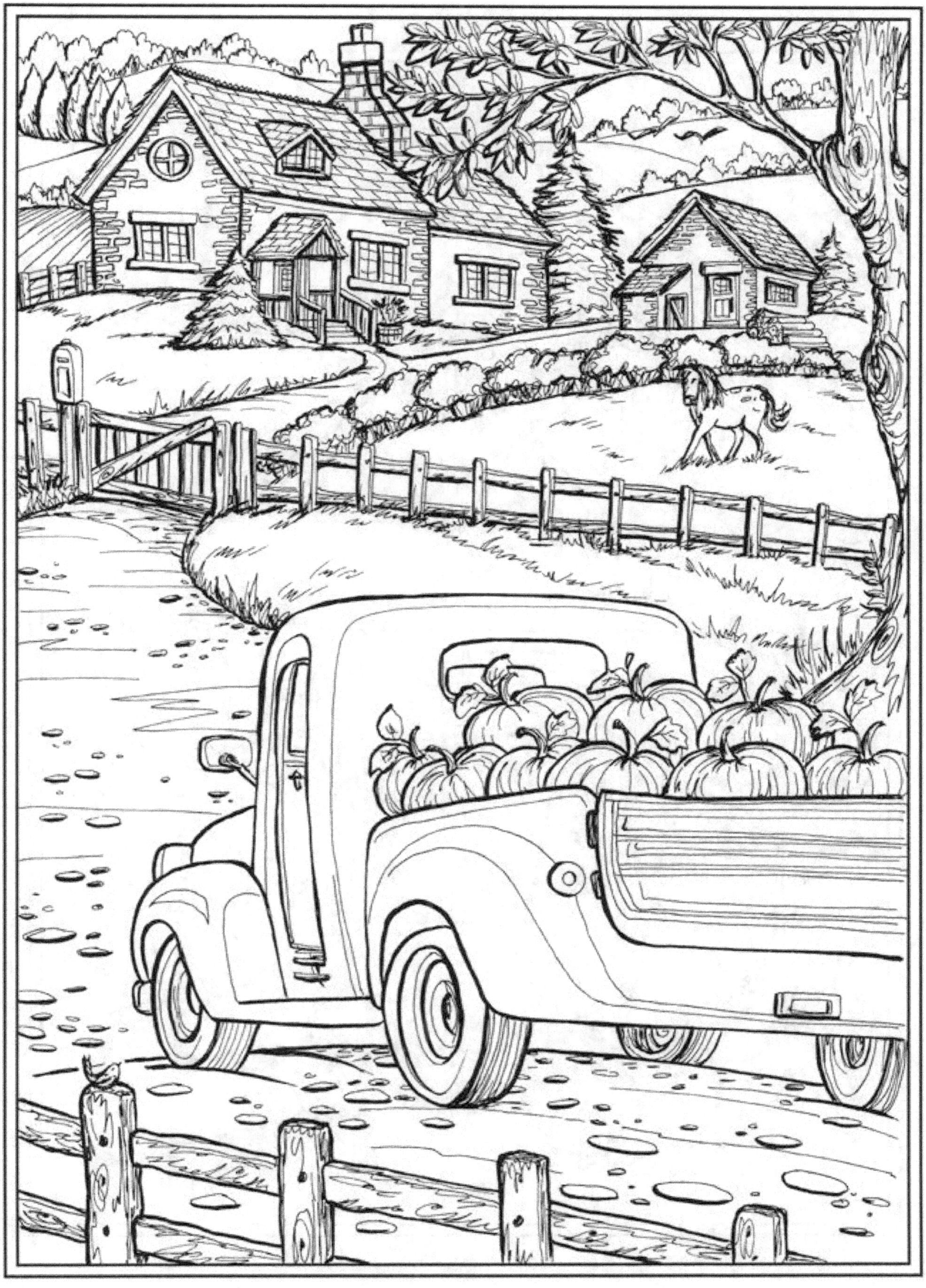

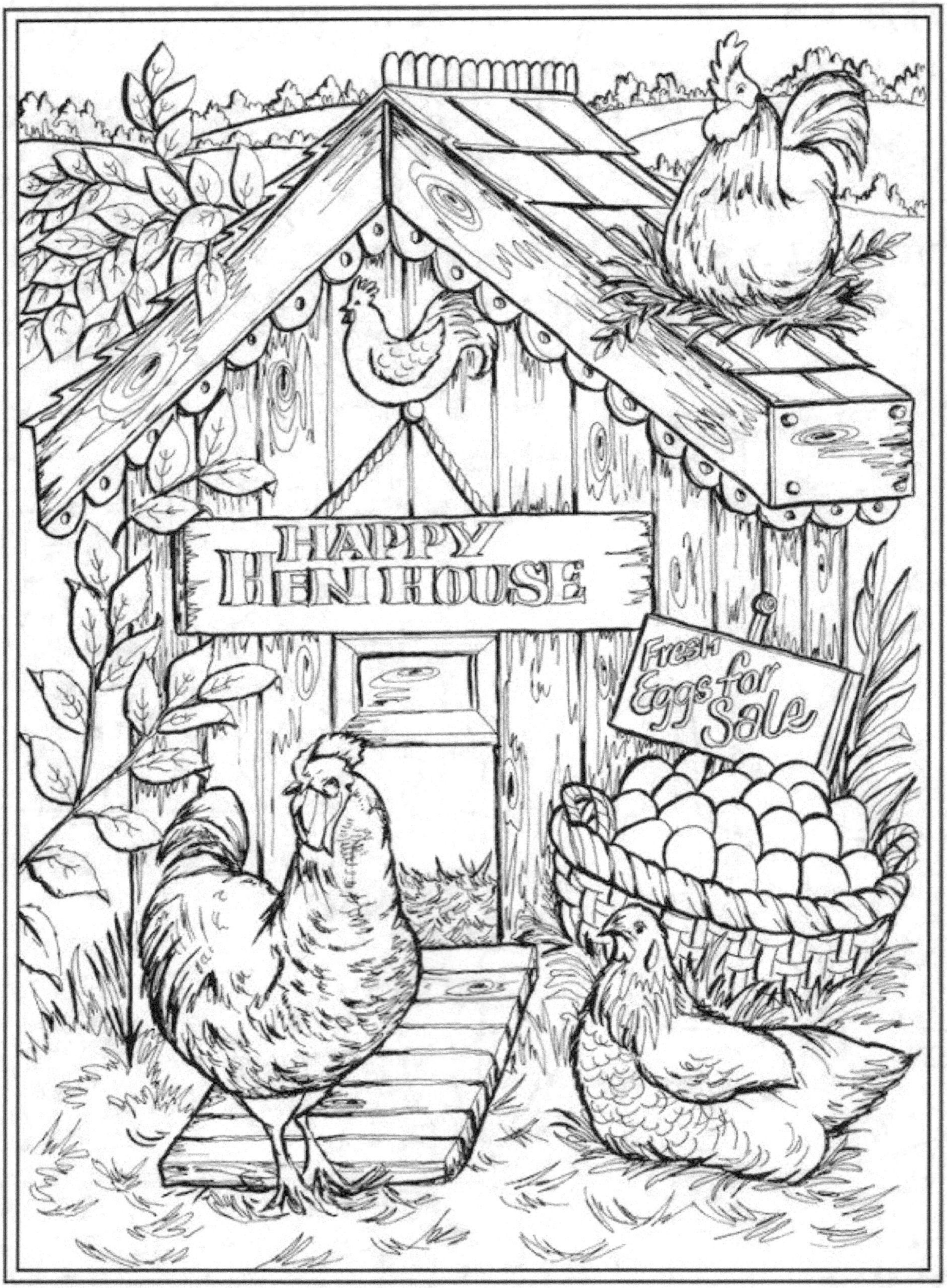
HAPPY
HEN HOUSE
Fresh
Eggs for
Sale

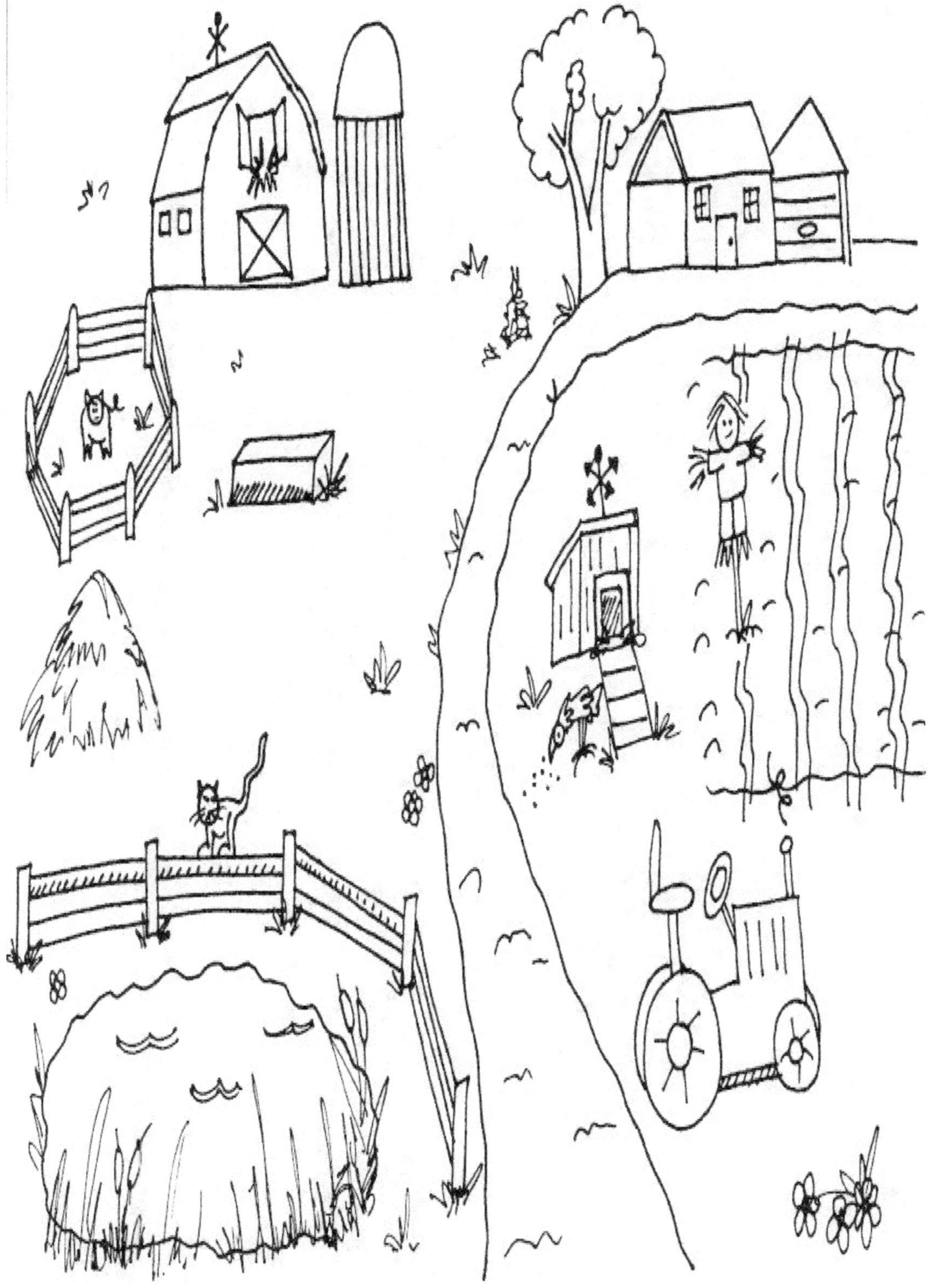

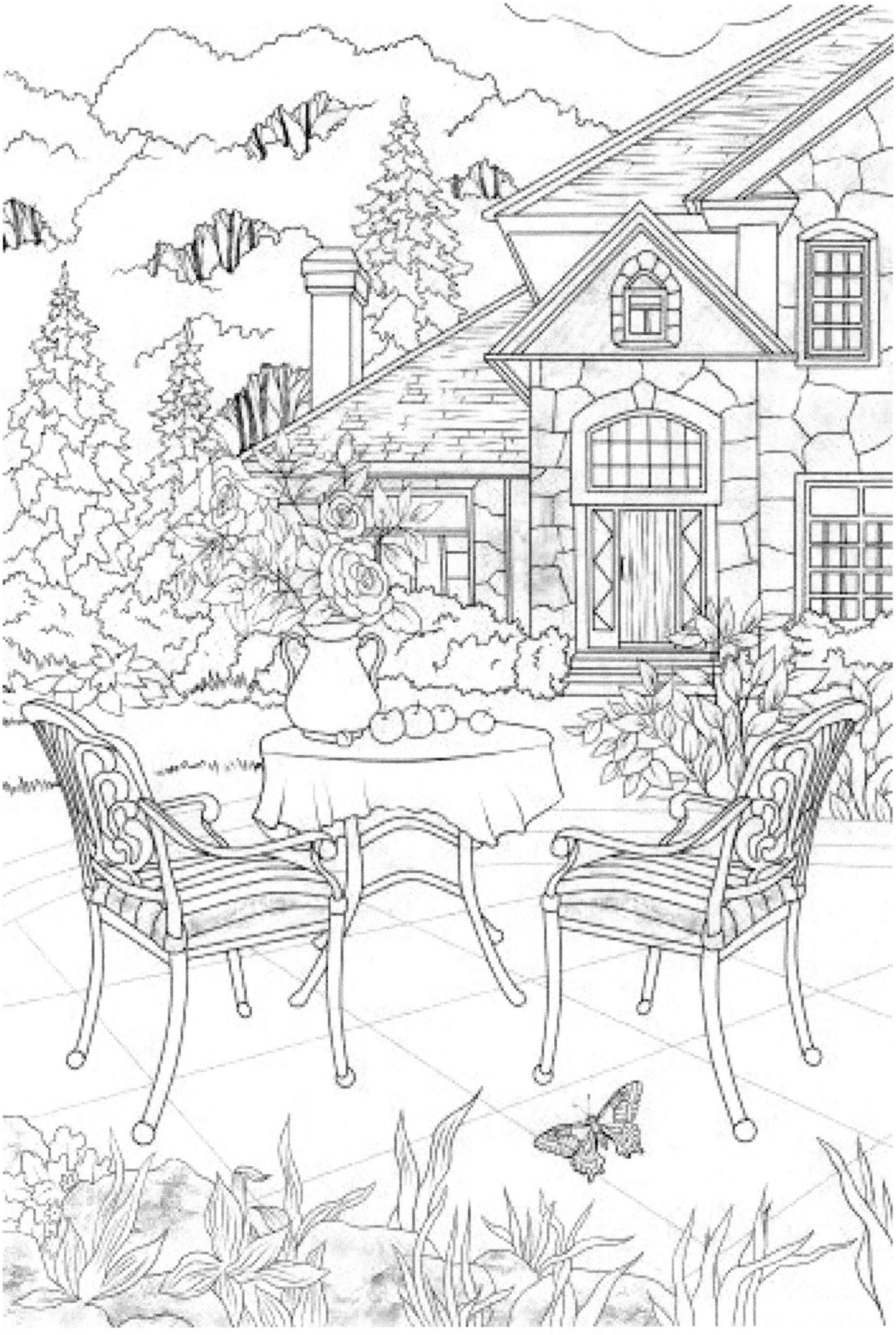

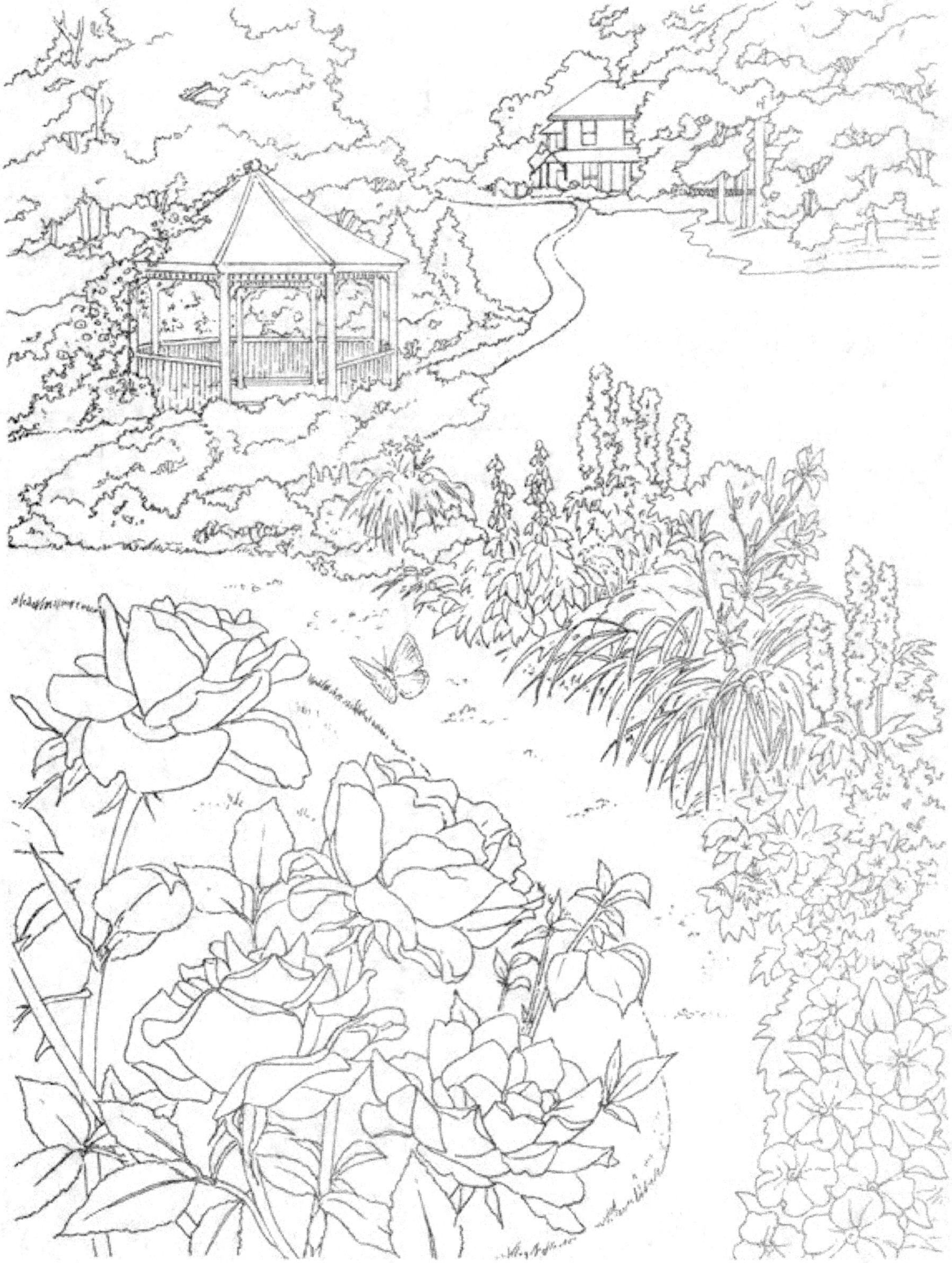

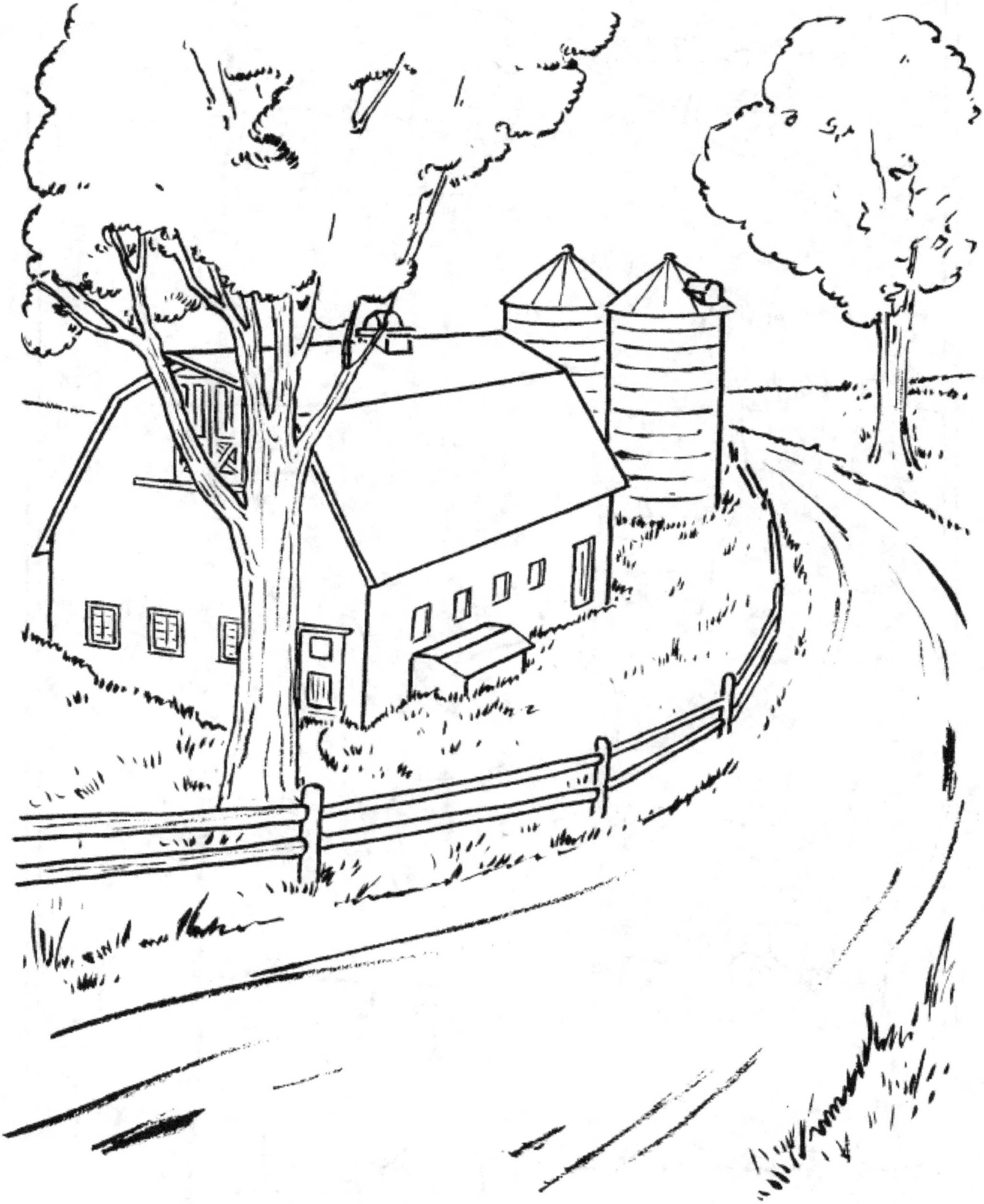

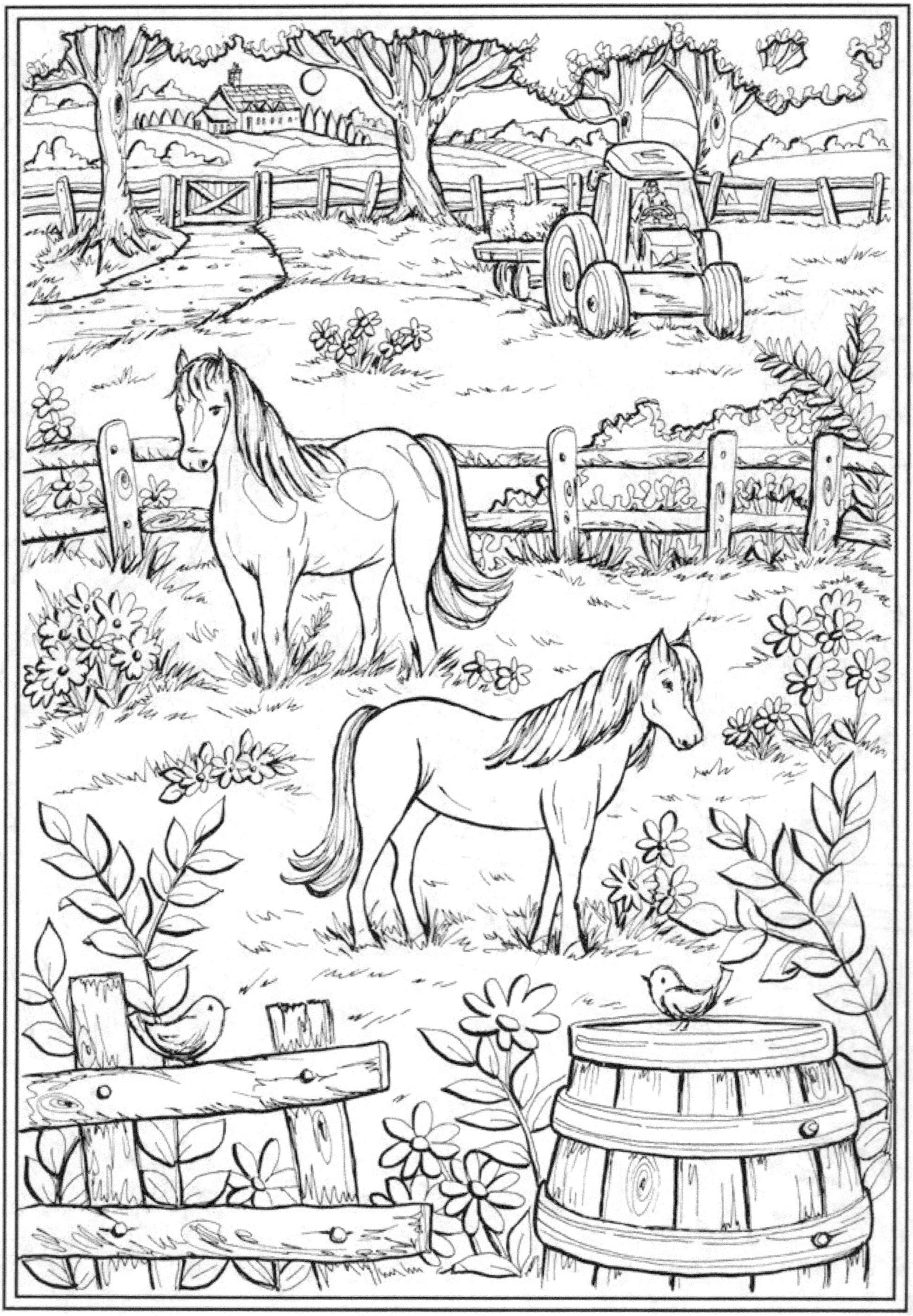

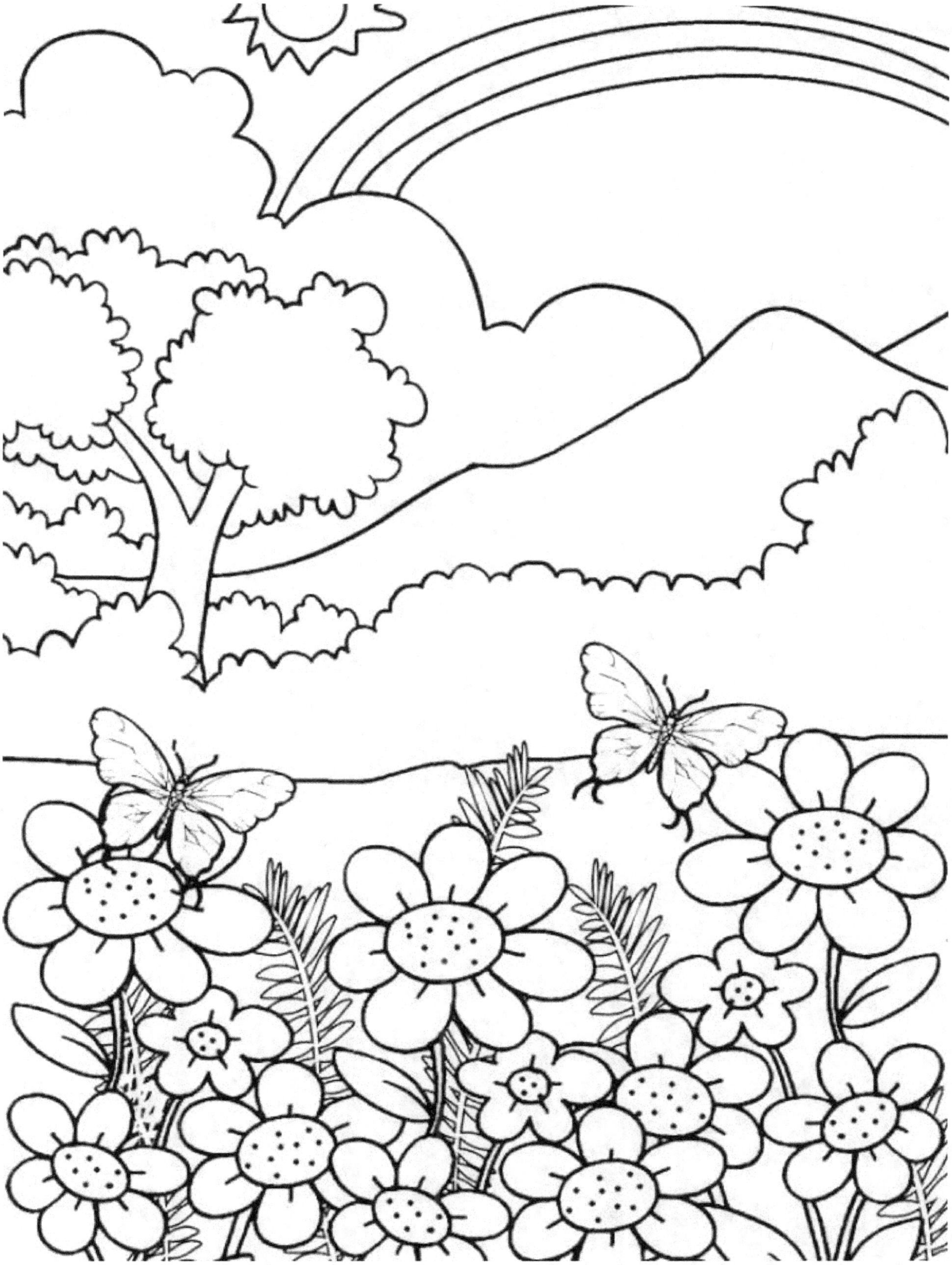

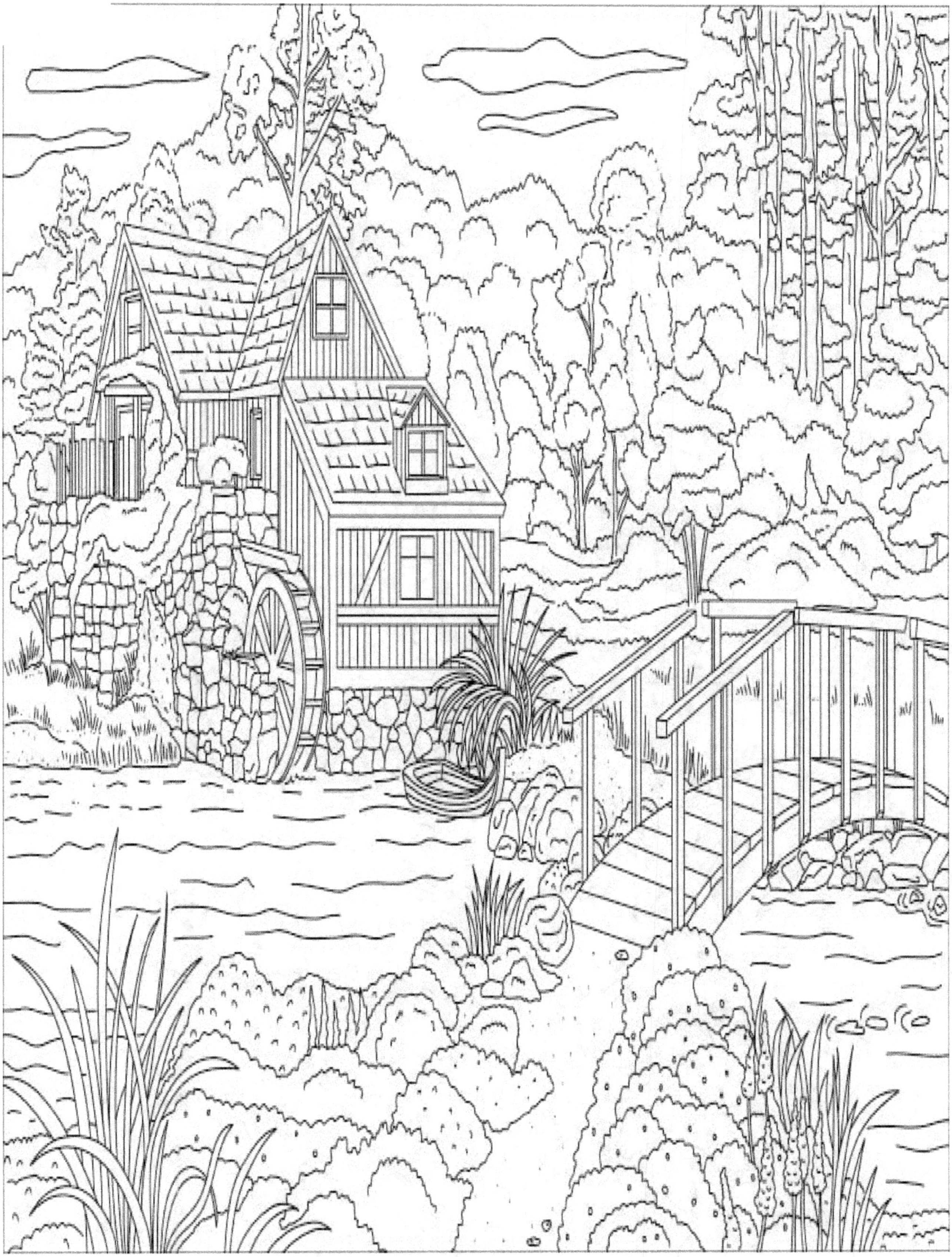

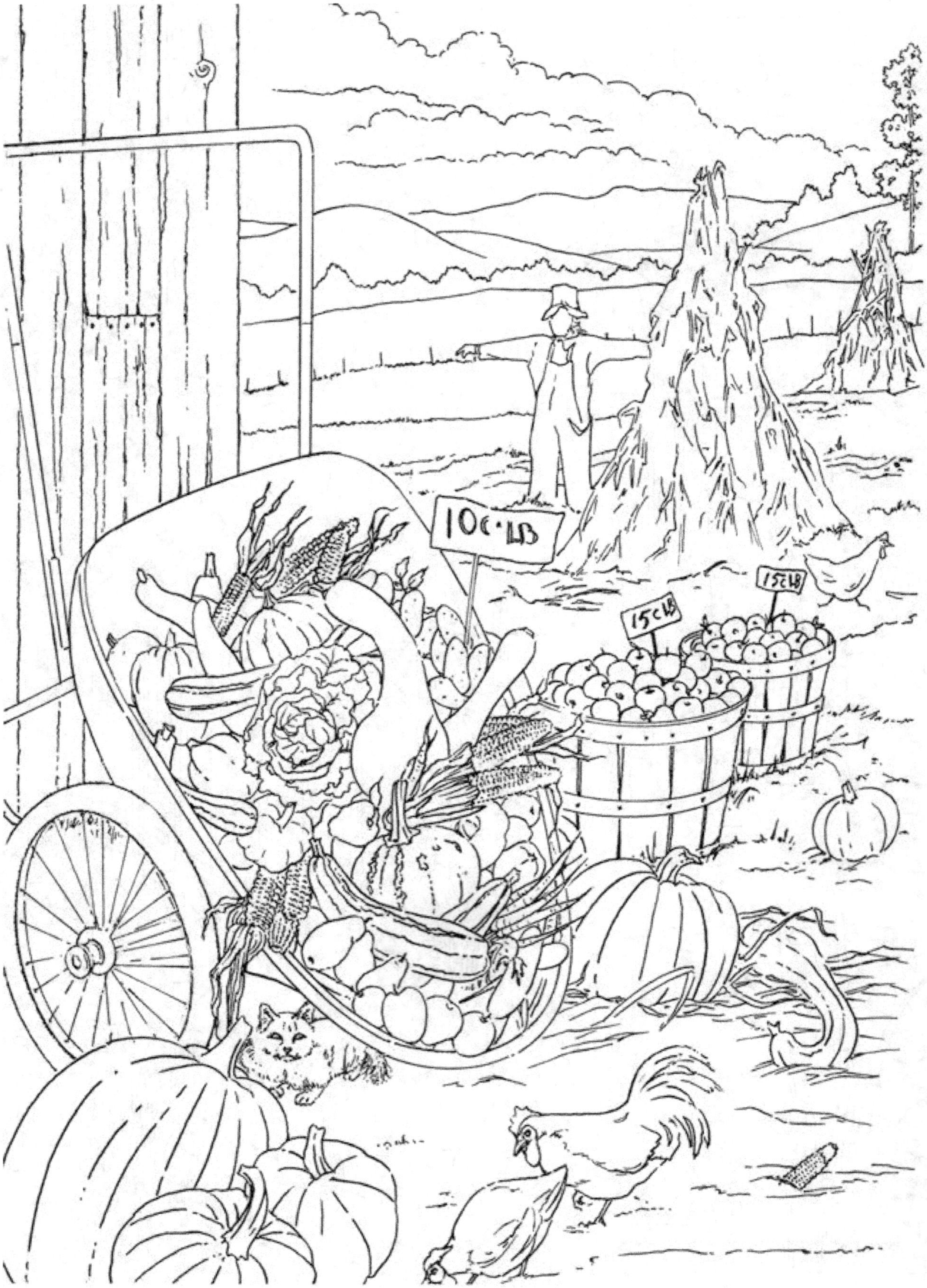
10c·LB
15cLB
15cLB

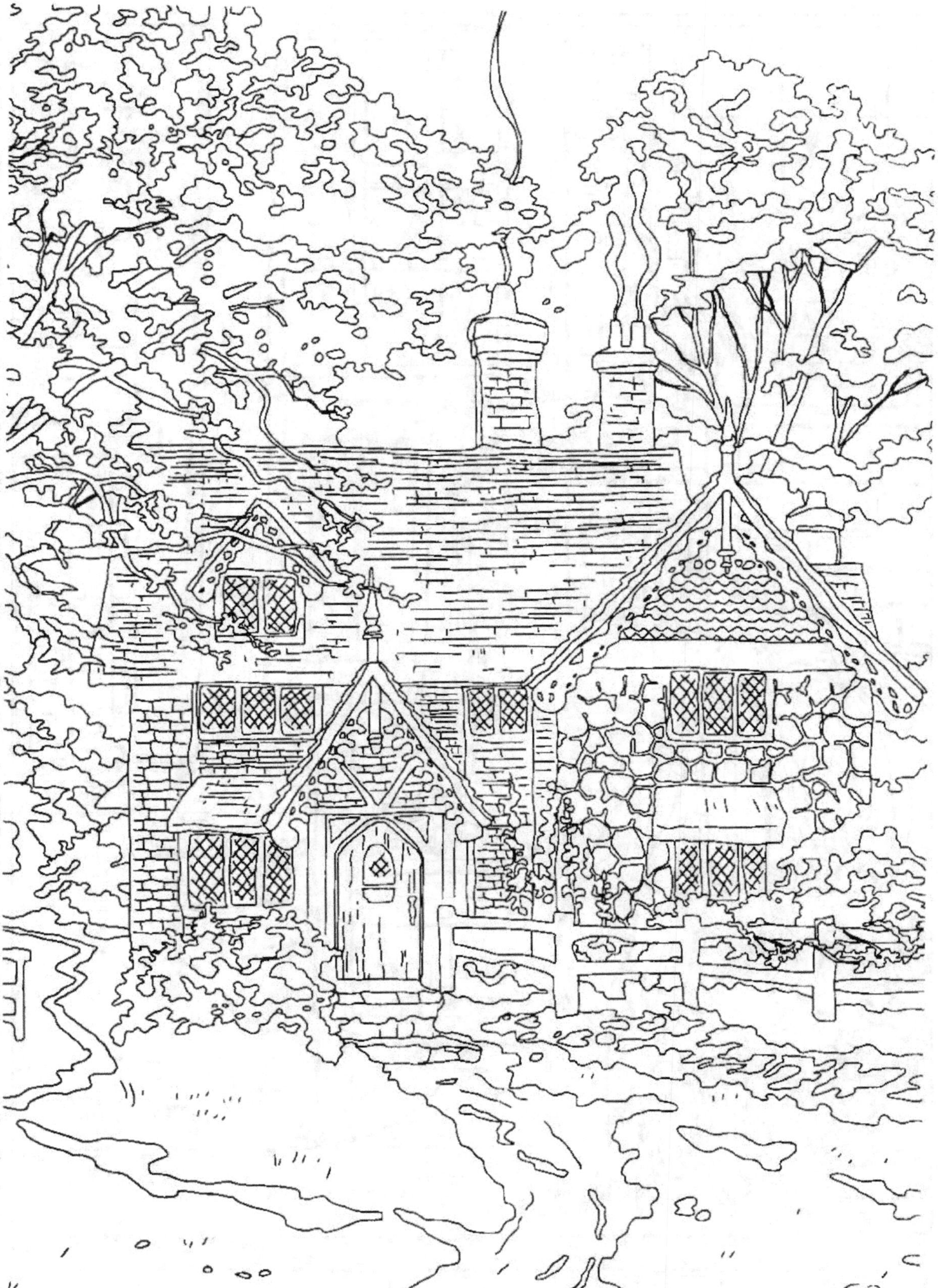
53

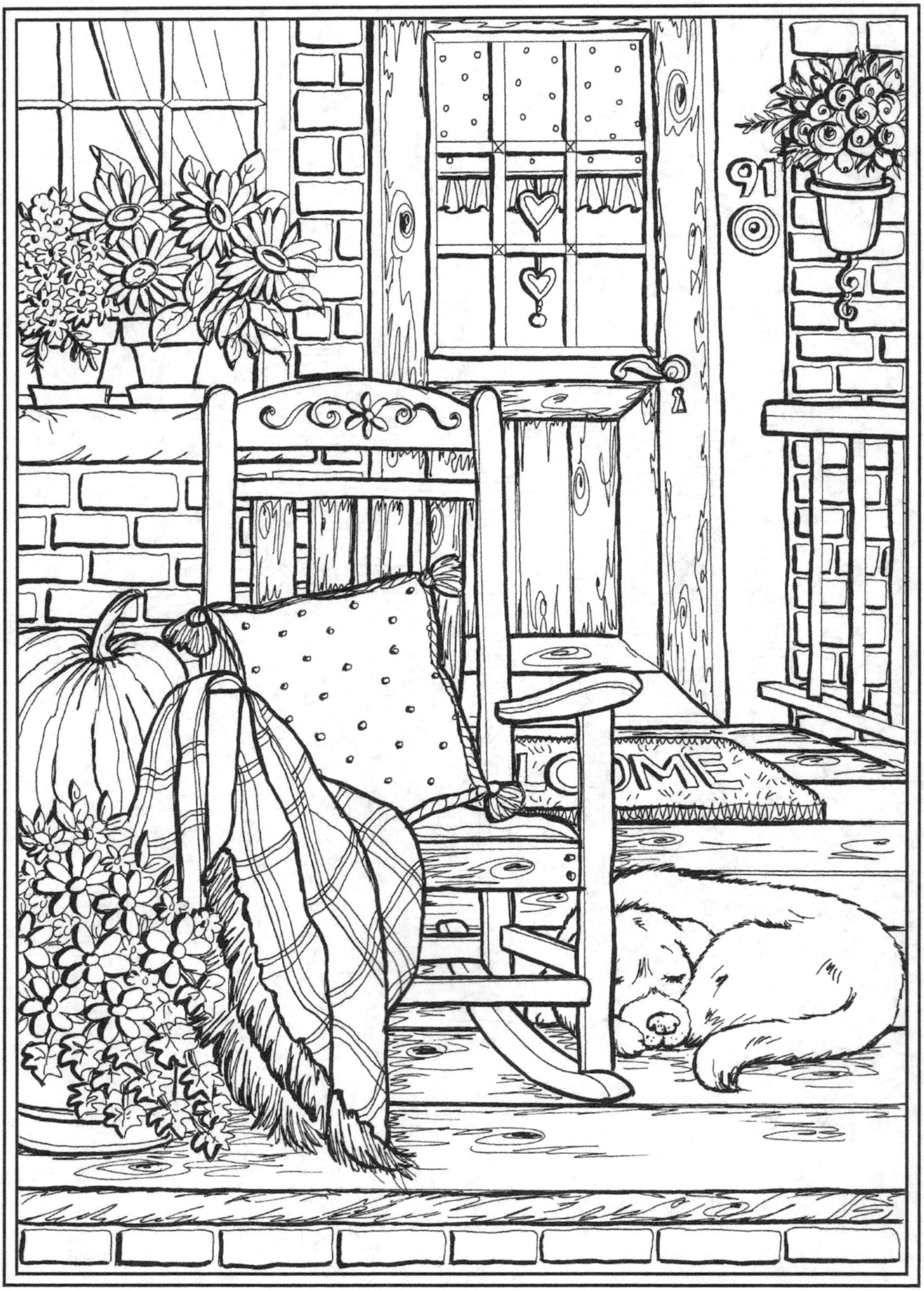
91
LCOME

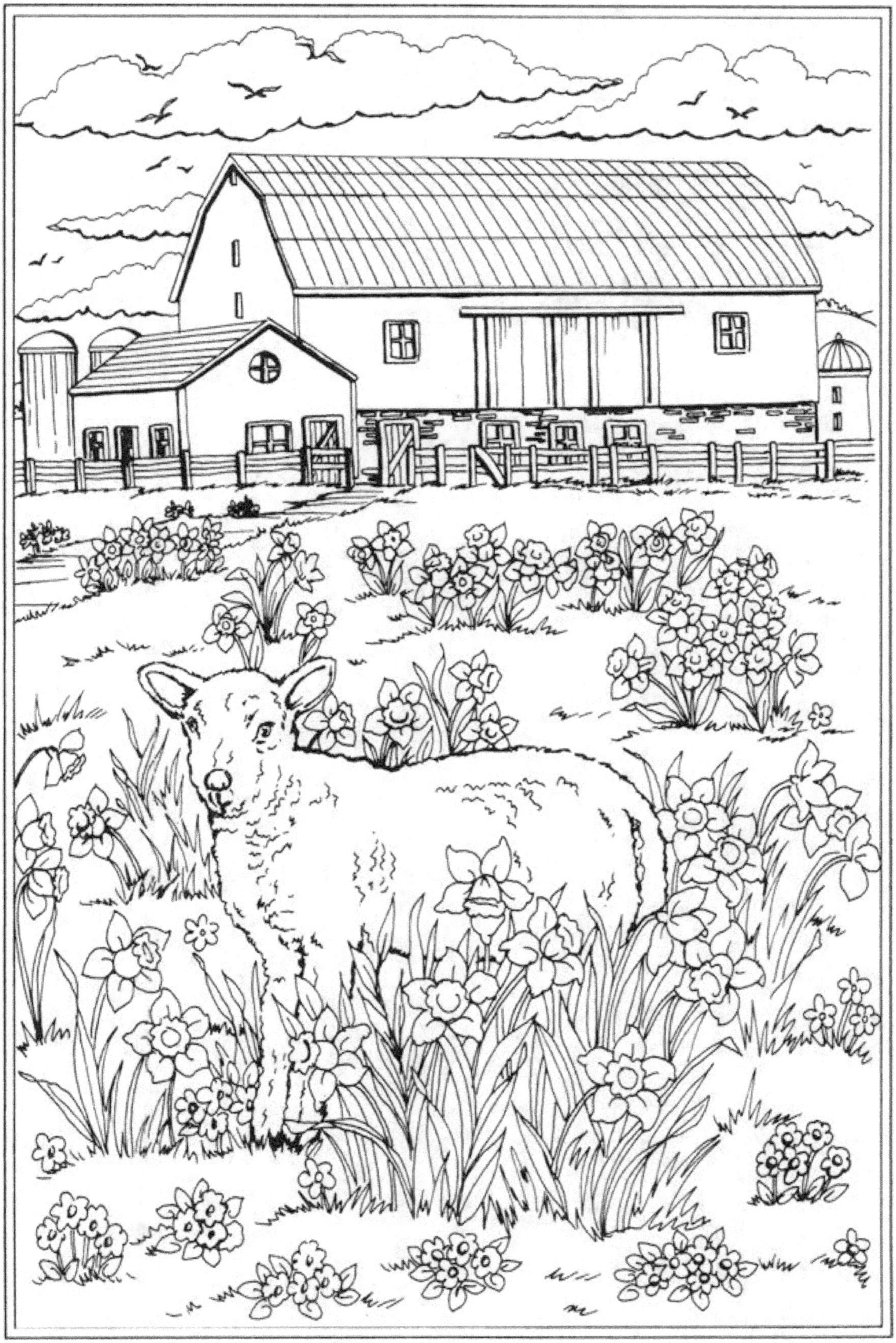

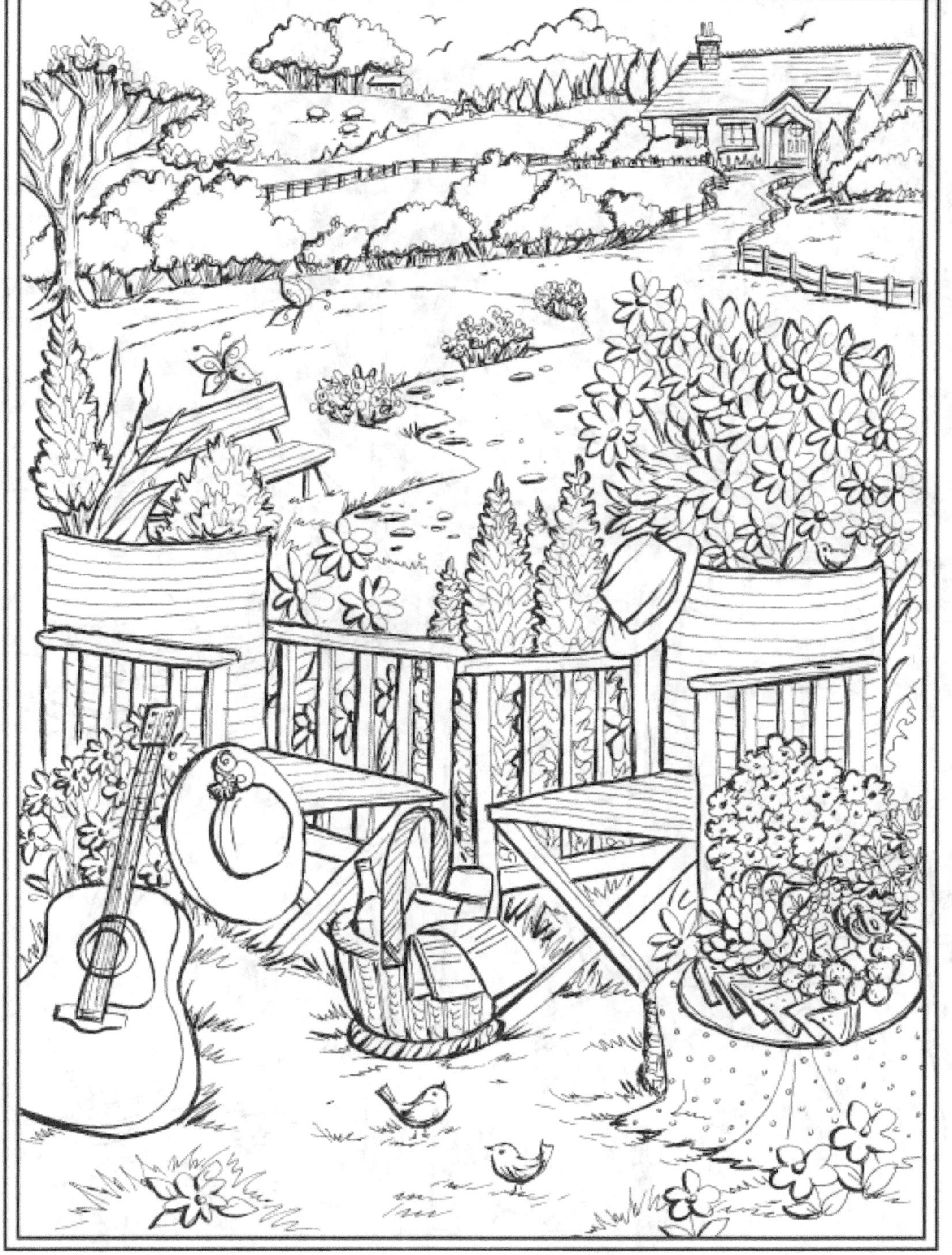

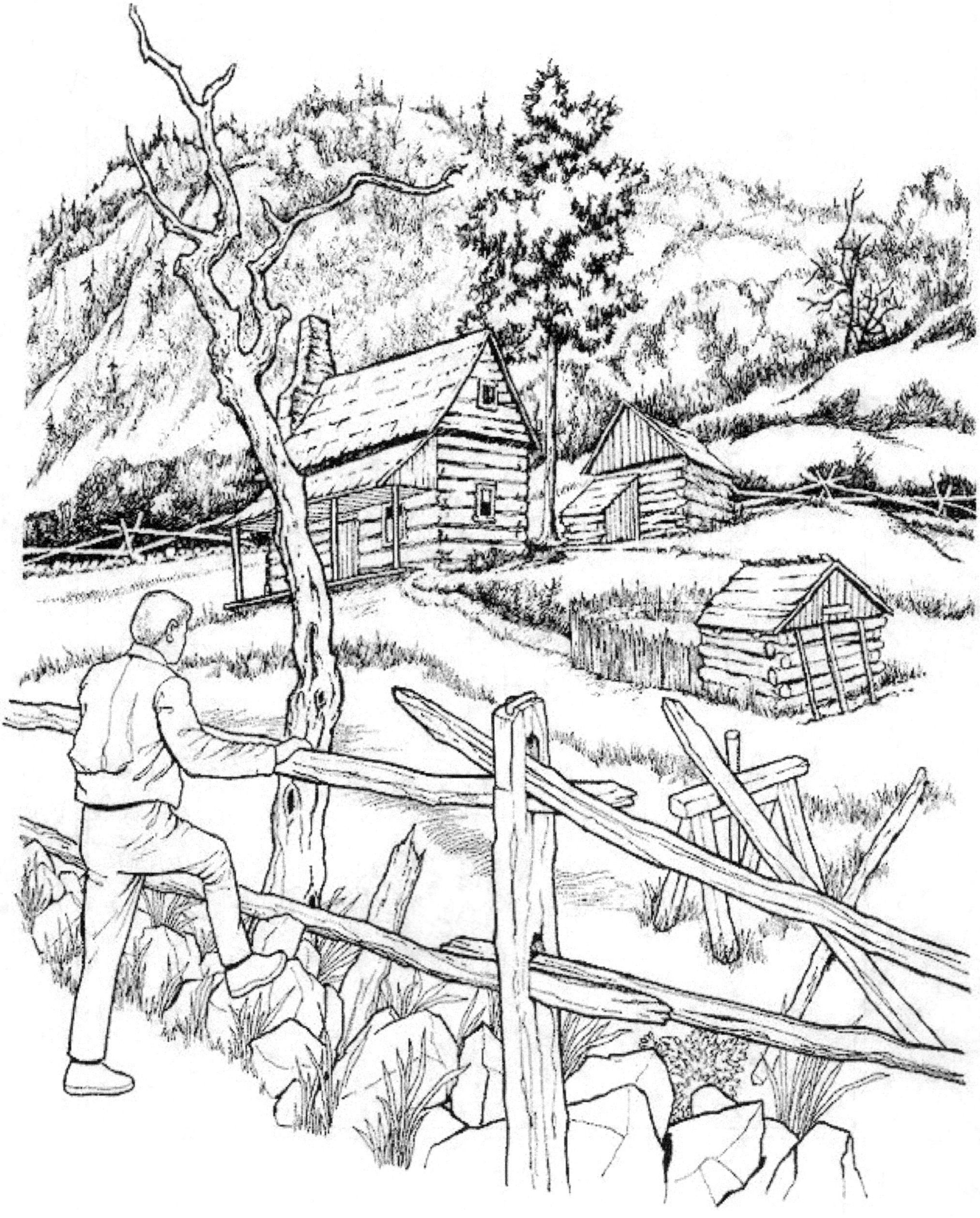

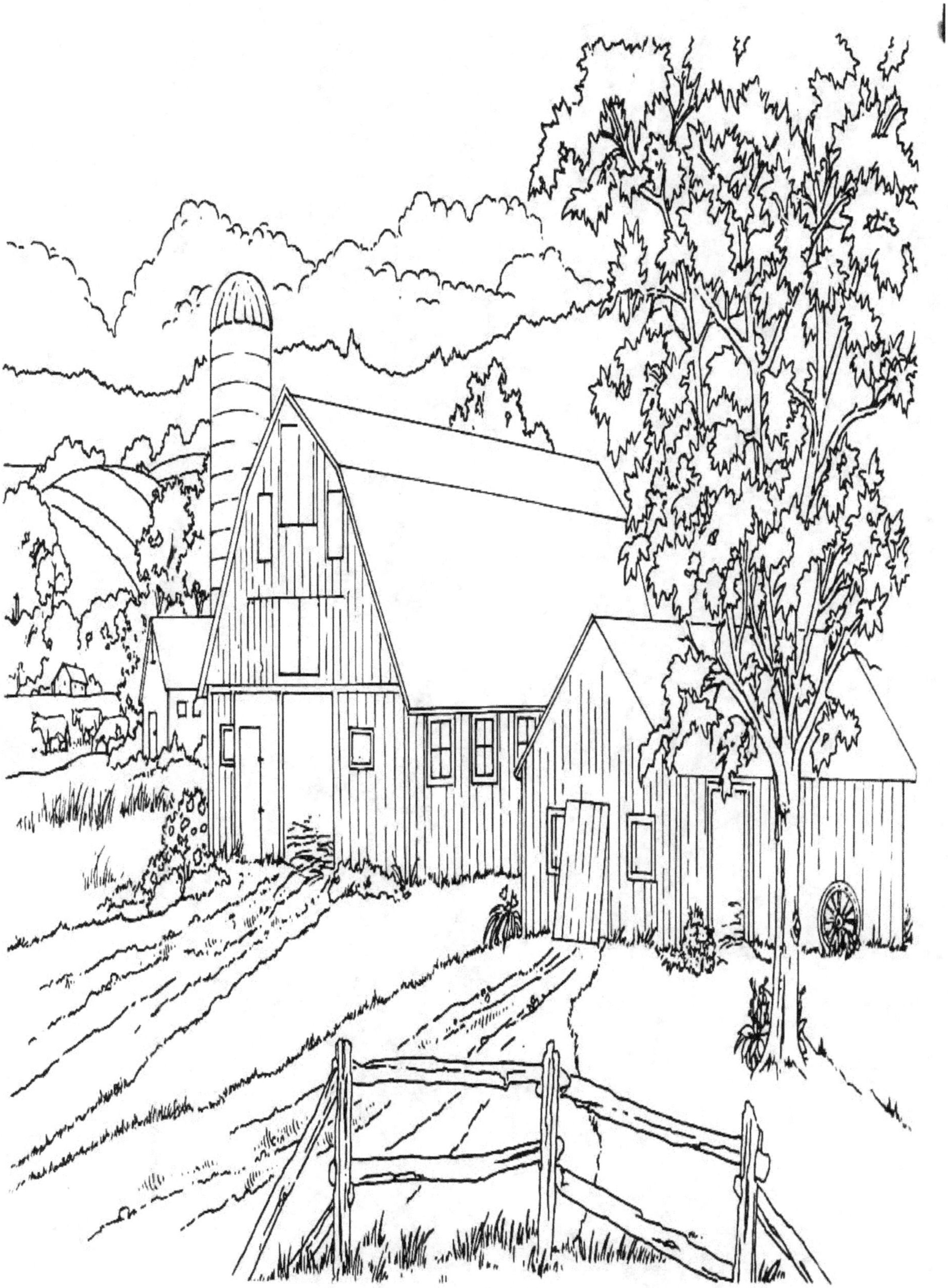

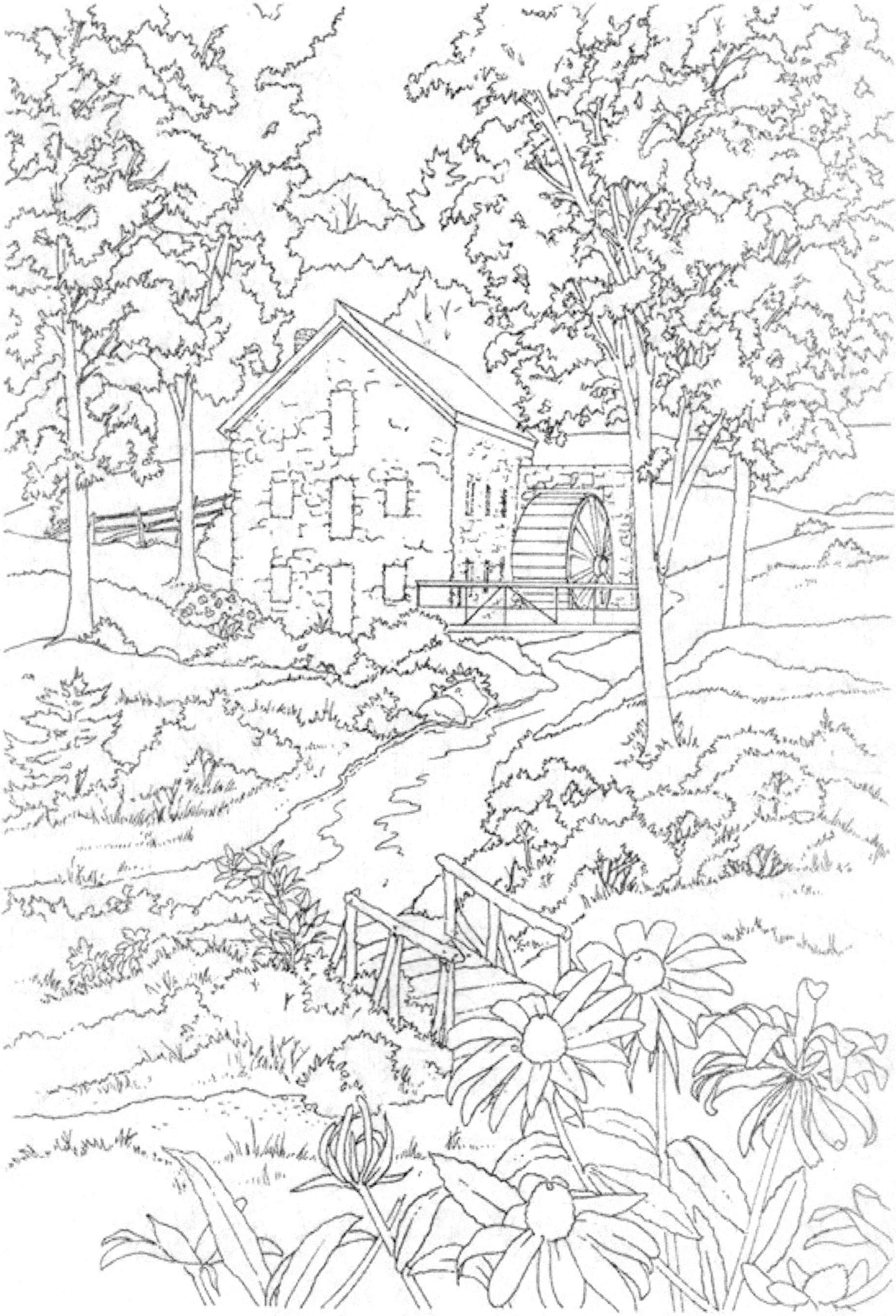

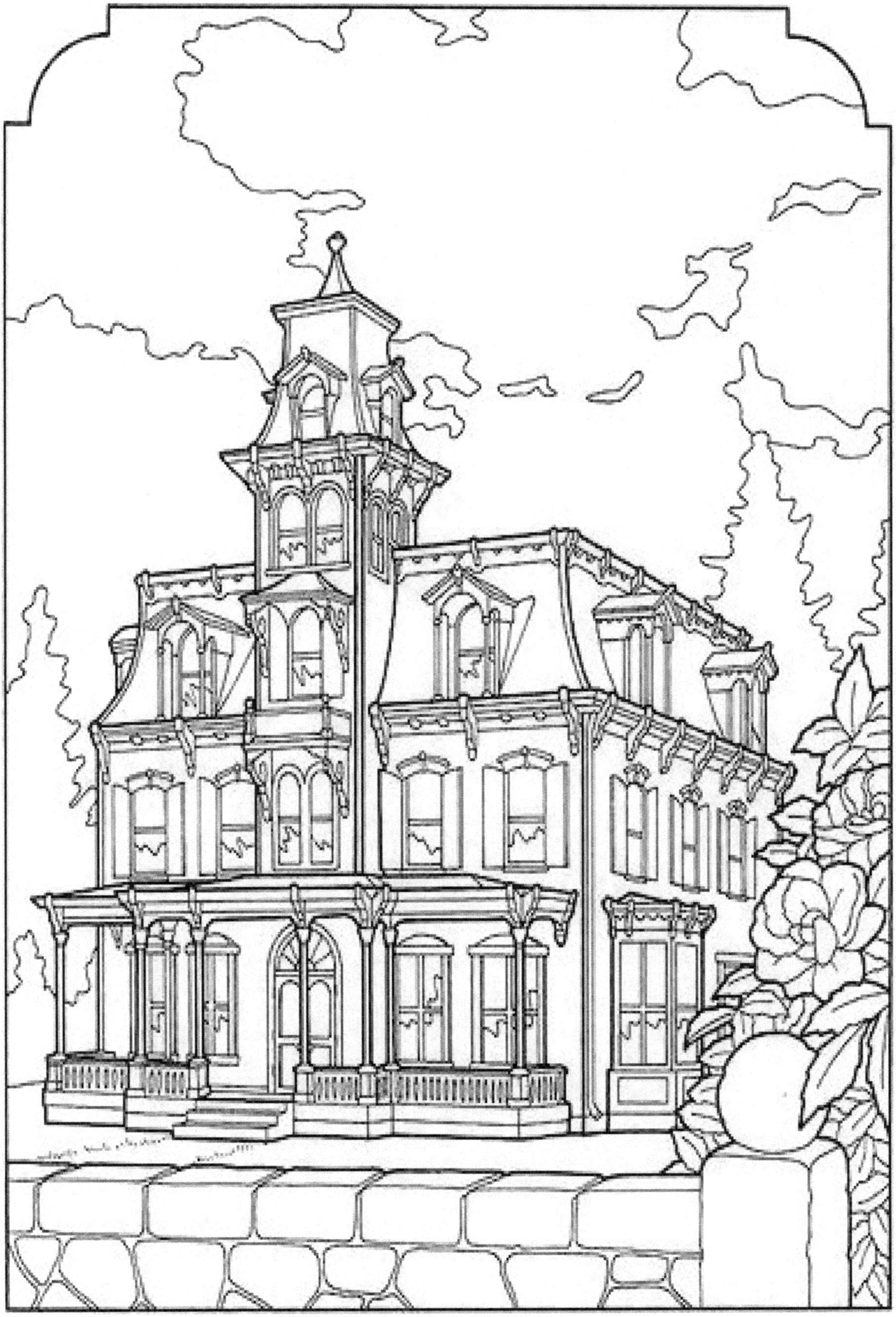

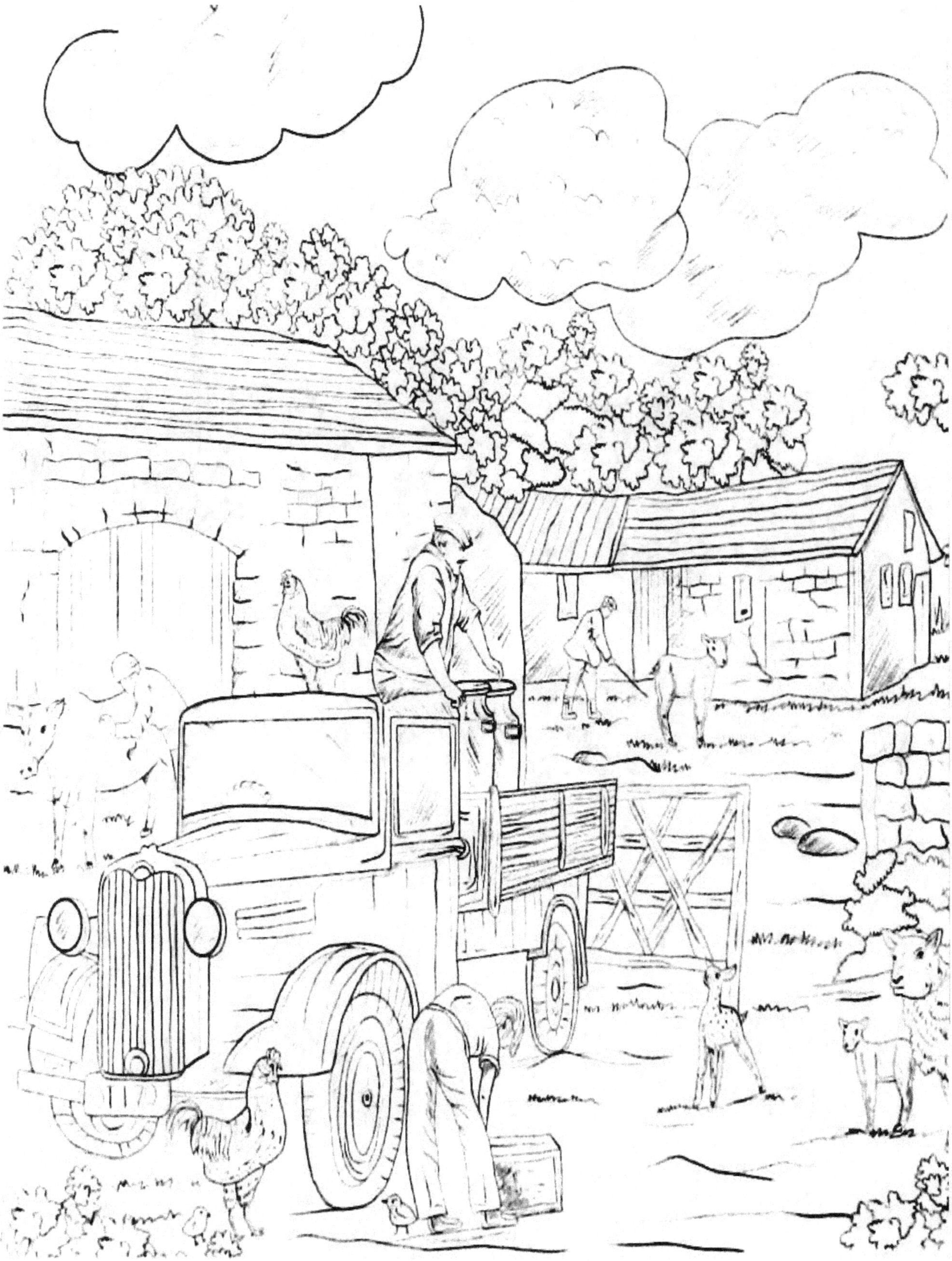

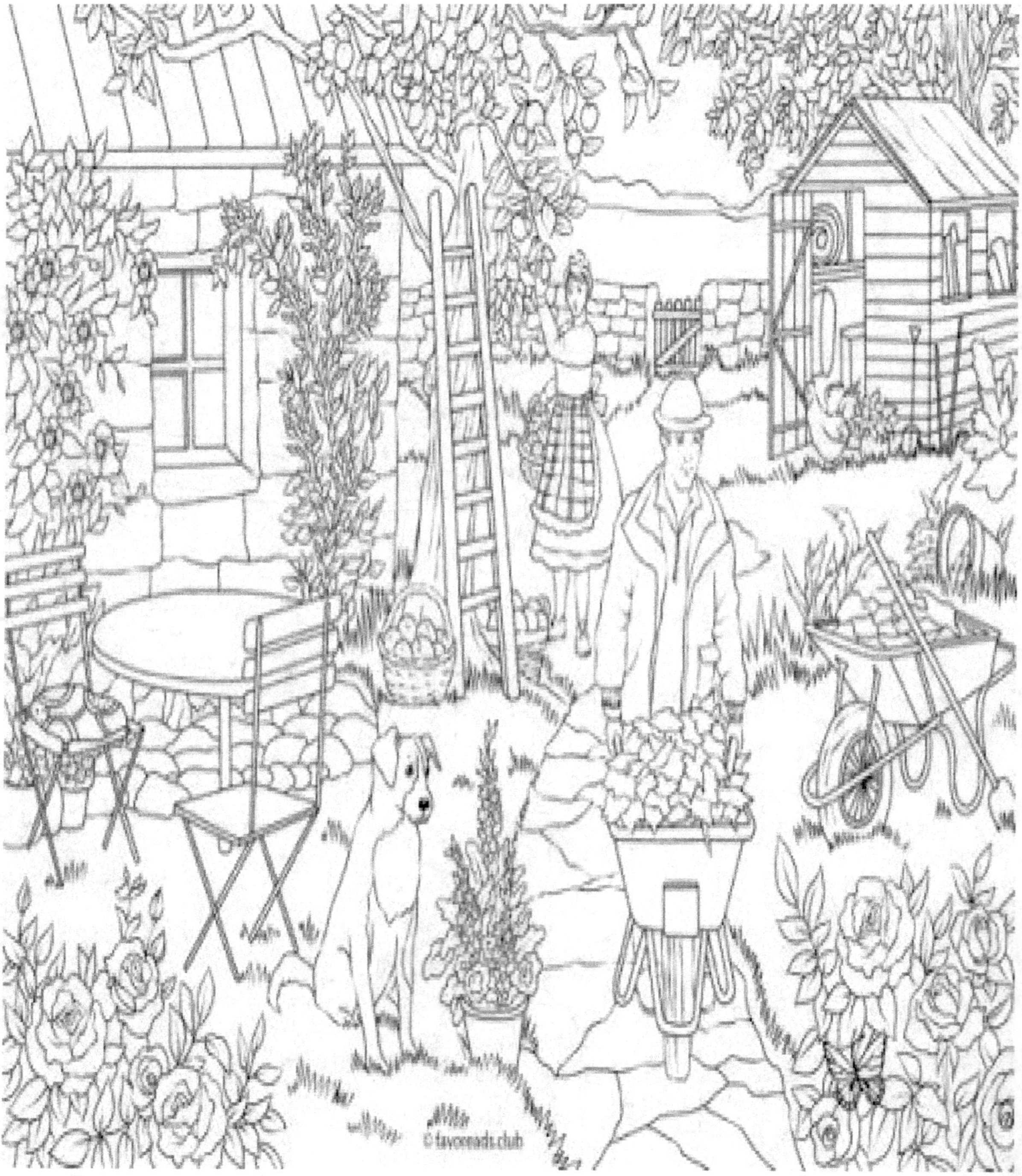
© favoreads.club

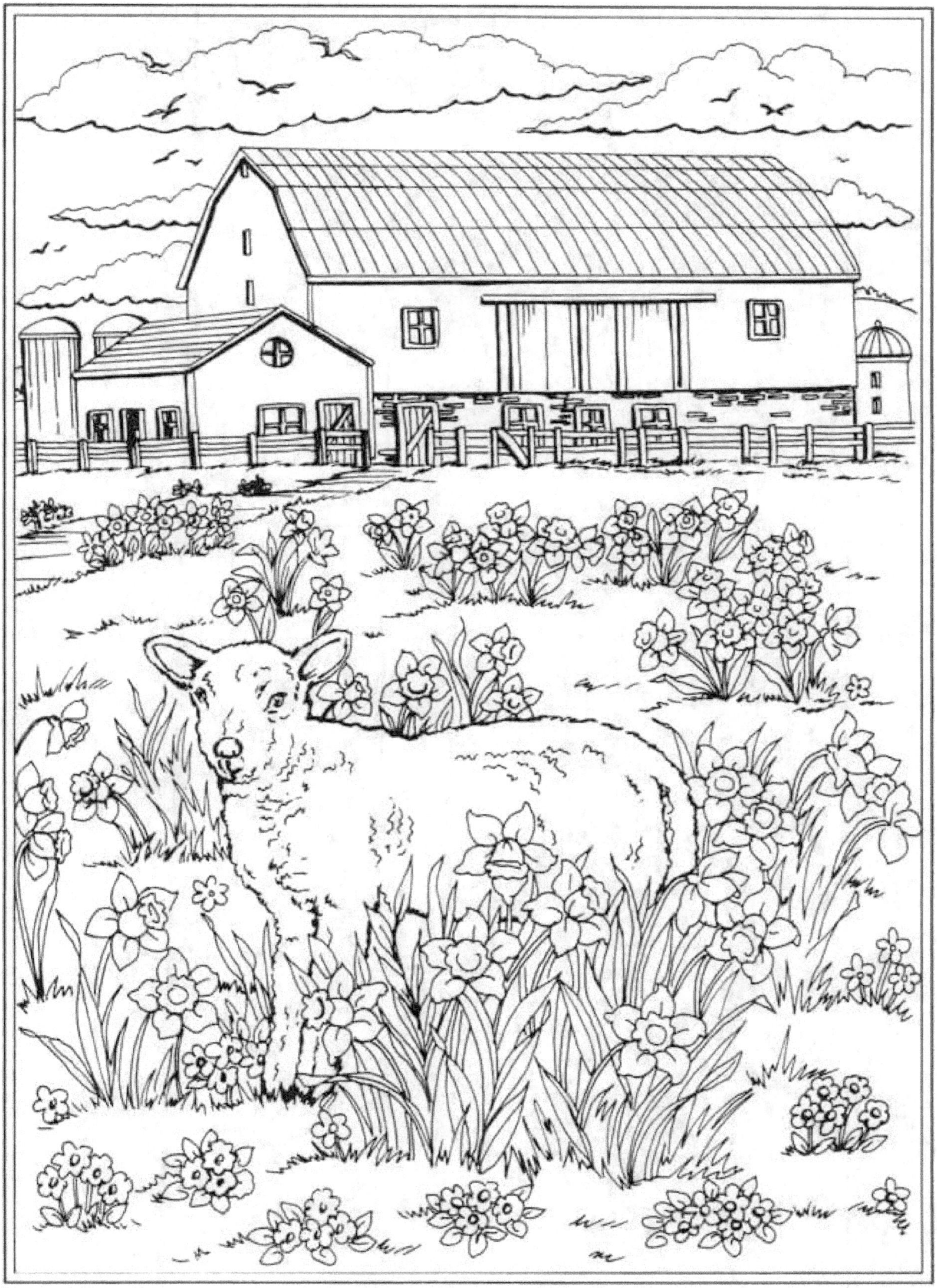

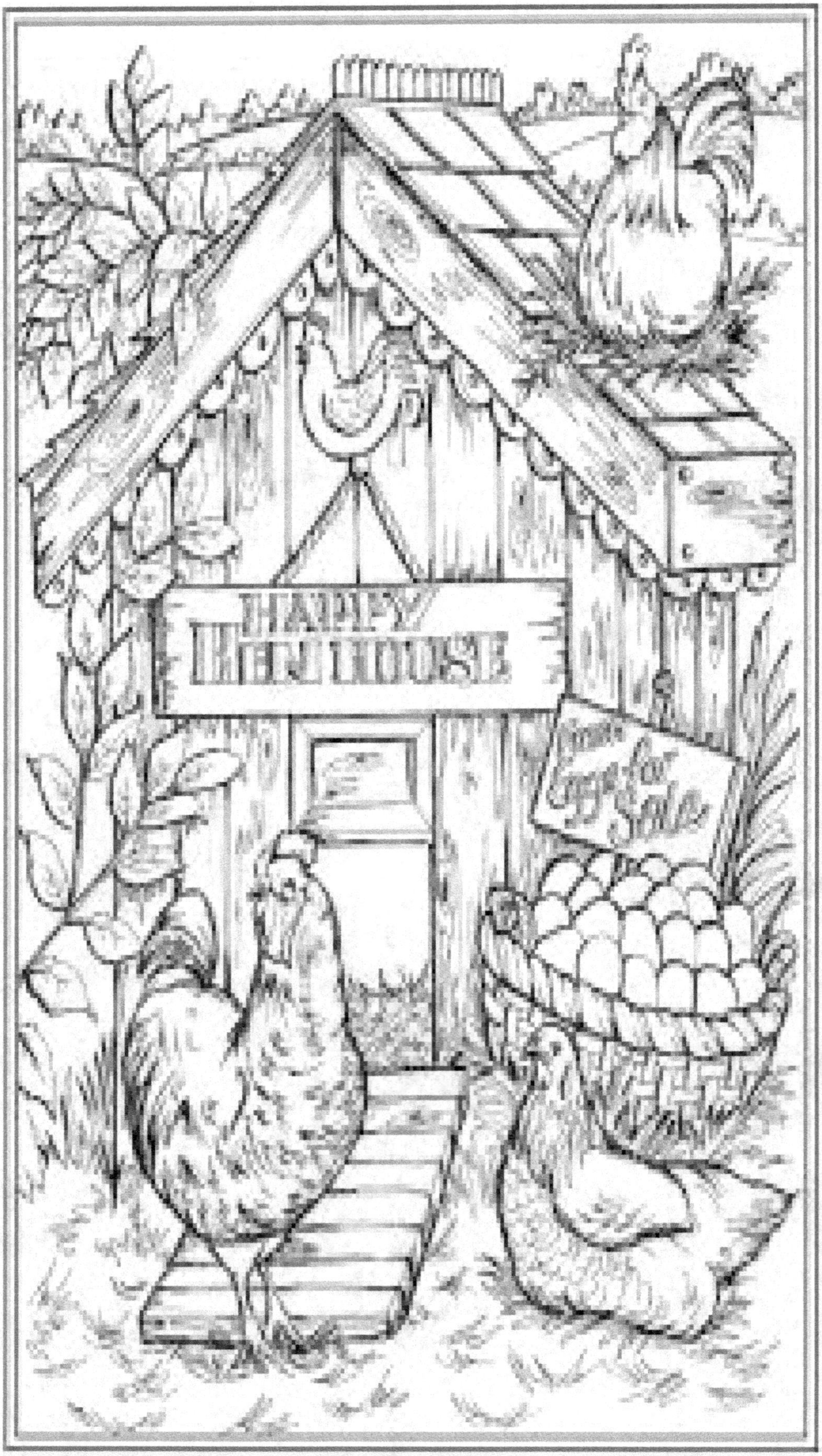
HAPPY
HEN HOUSE
Eggs for Sale

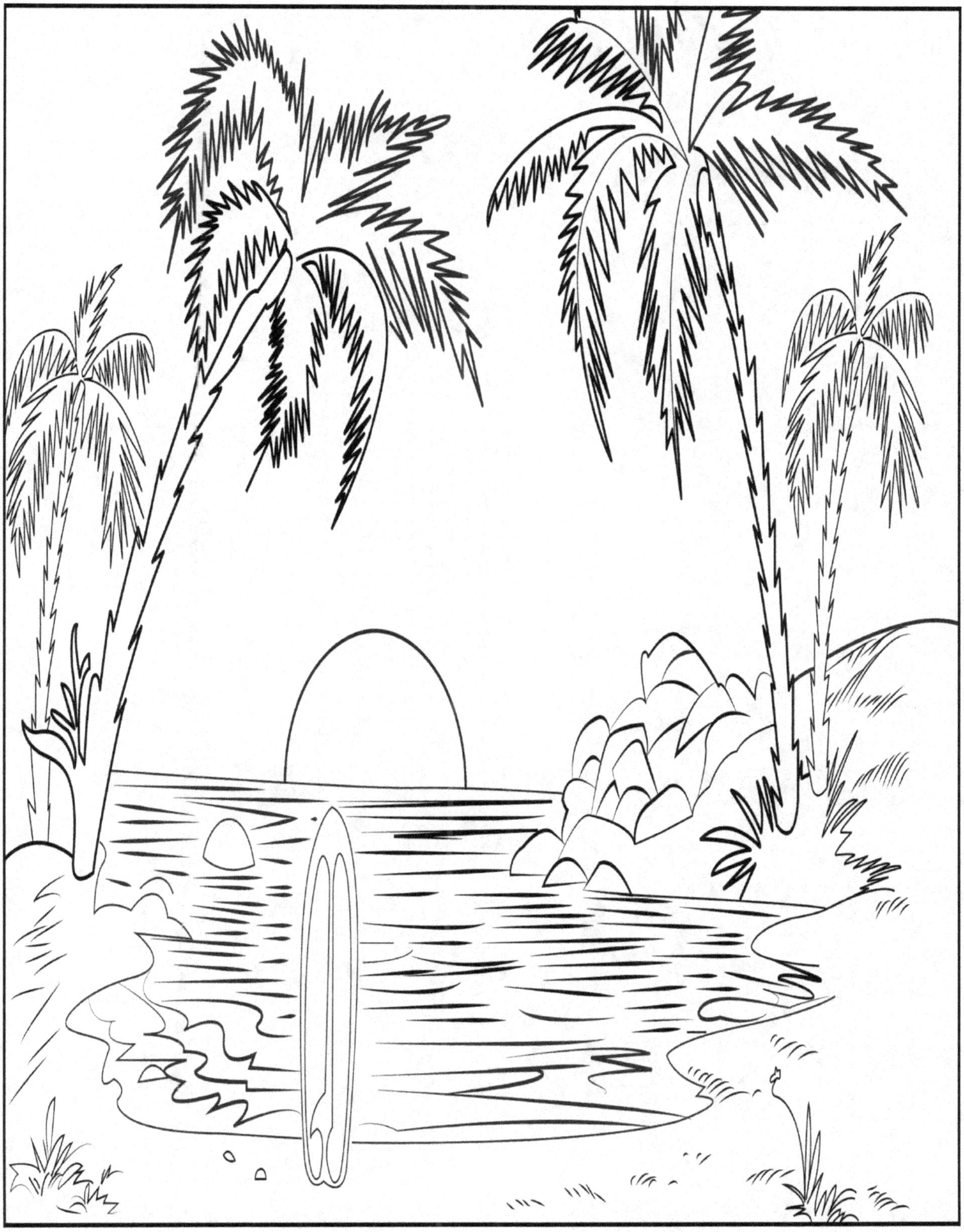

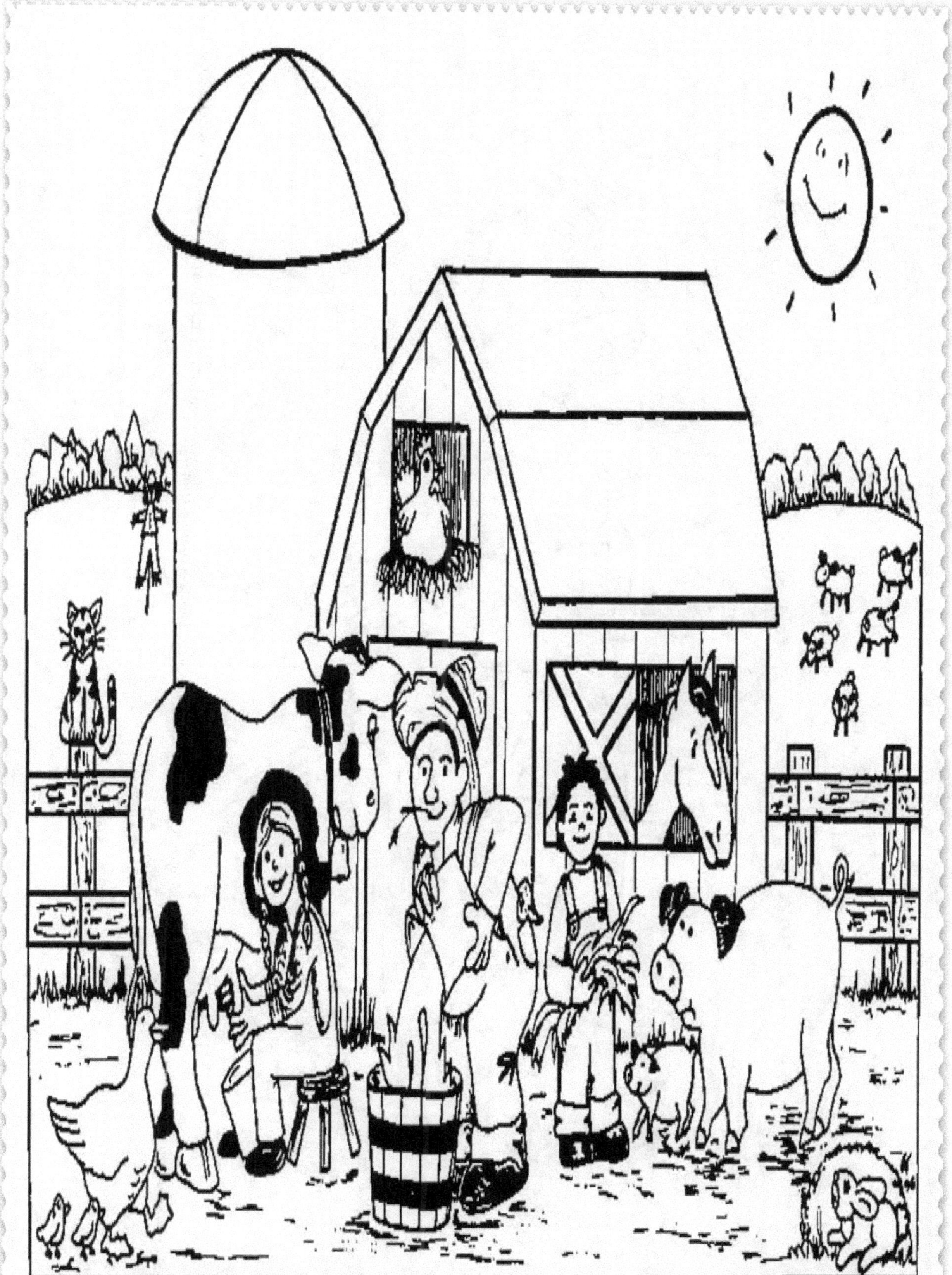

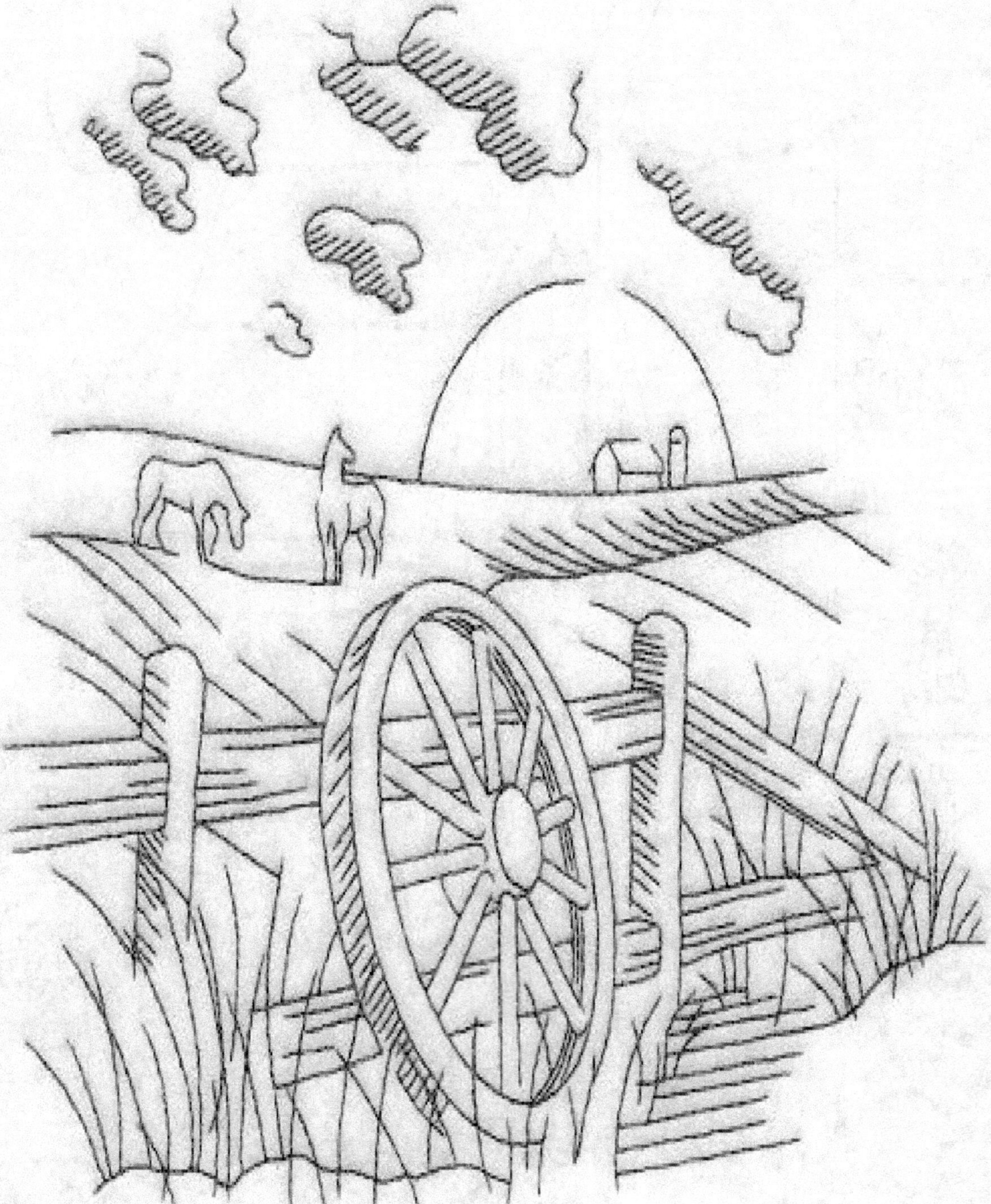

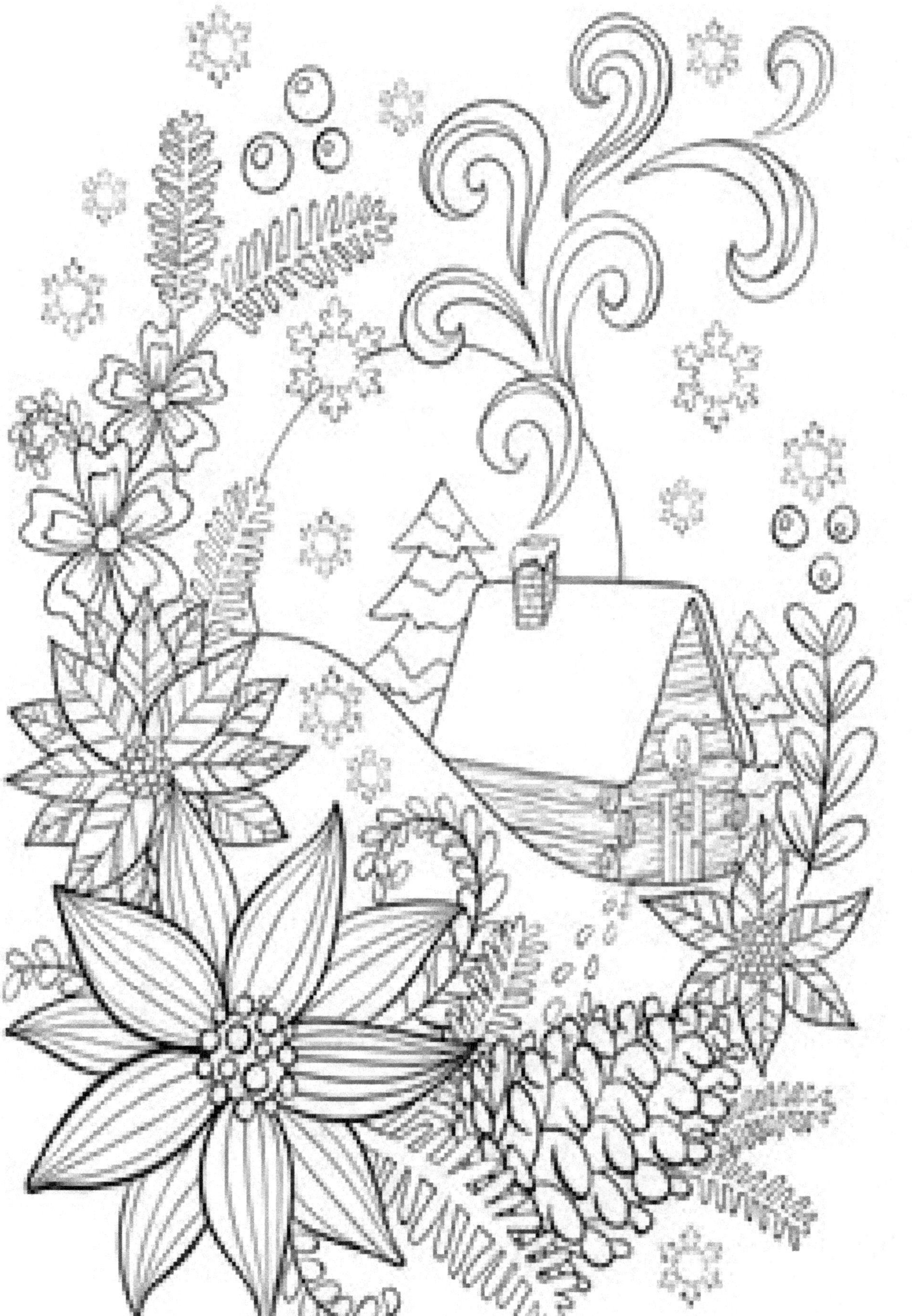

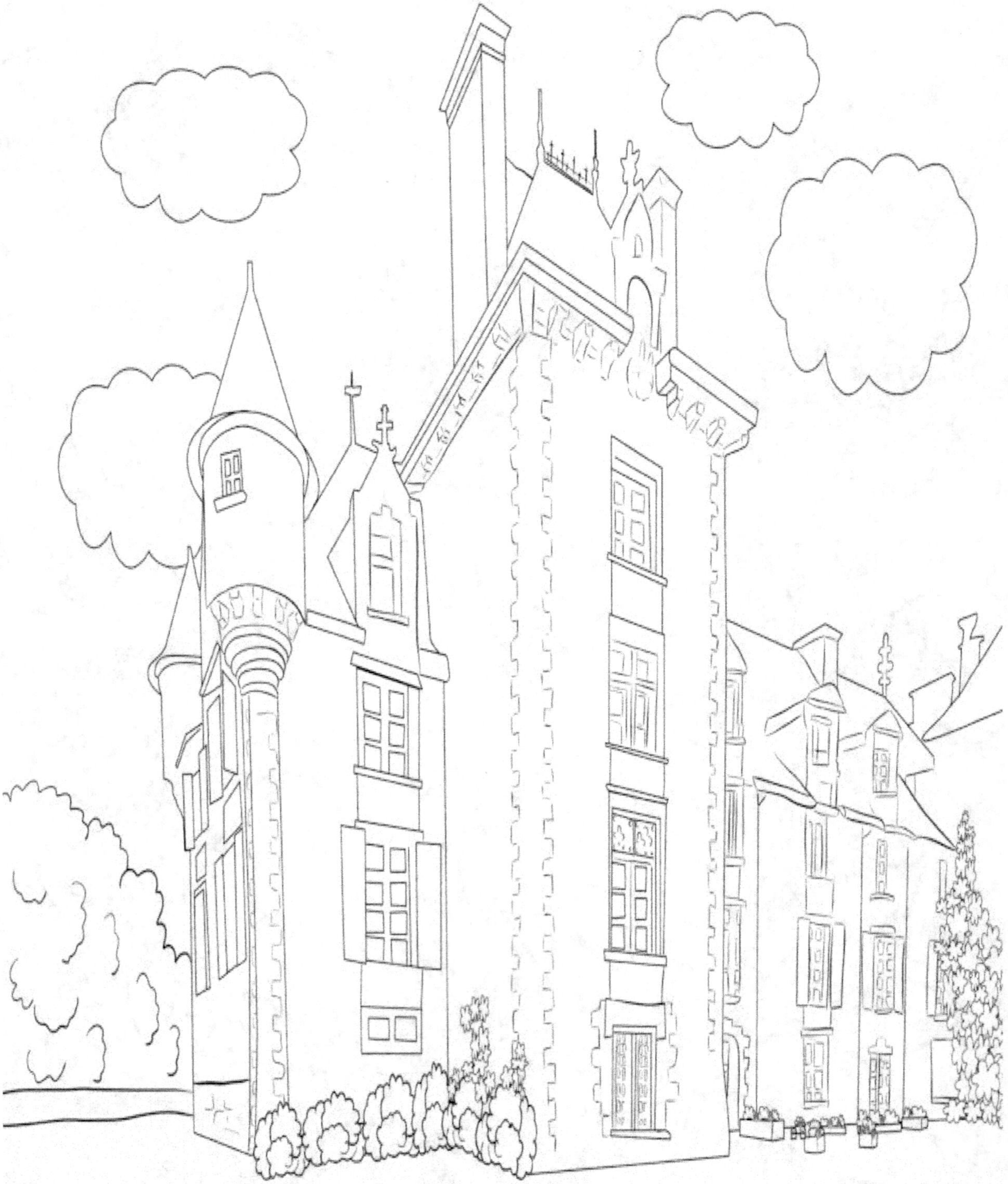

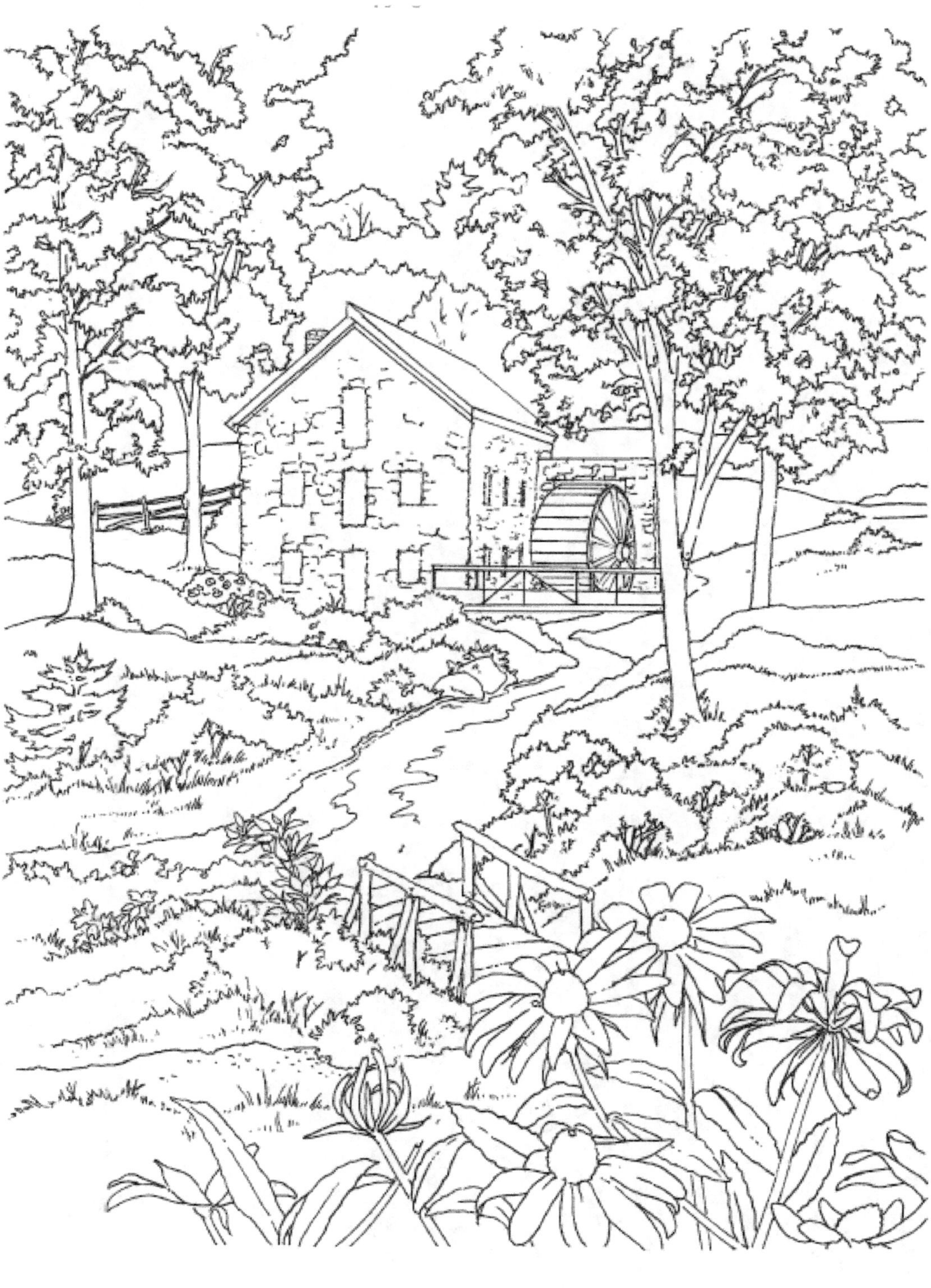

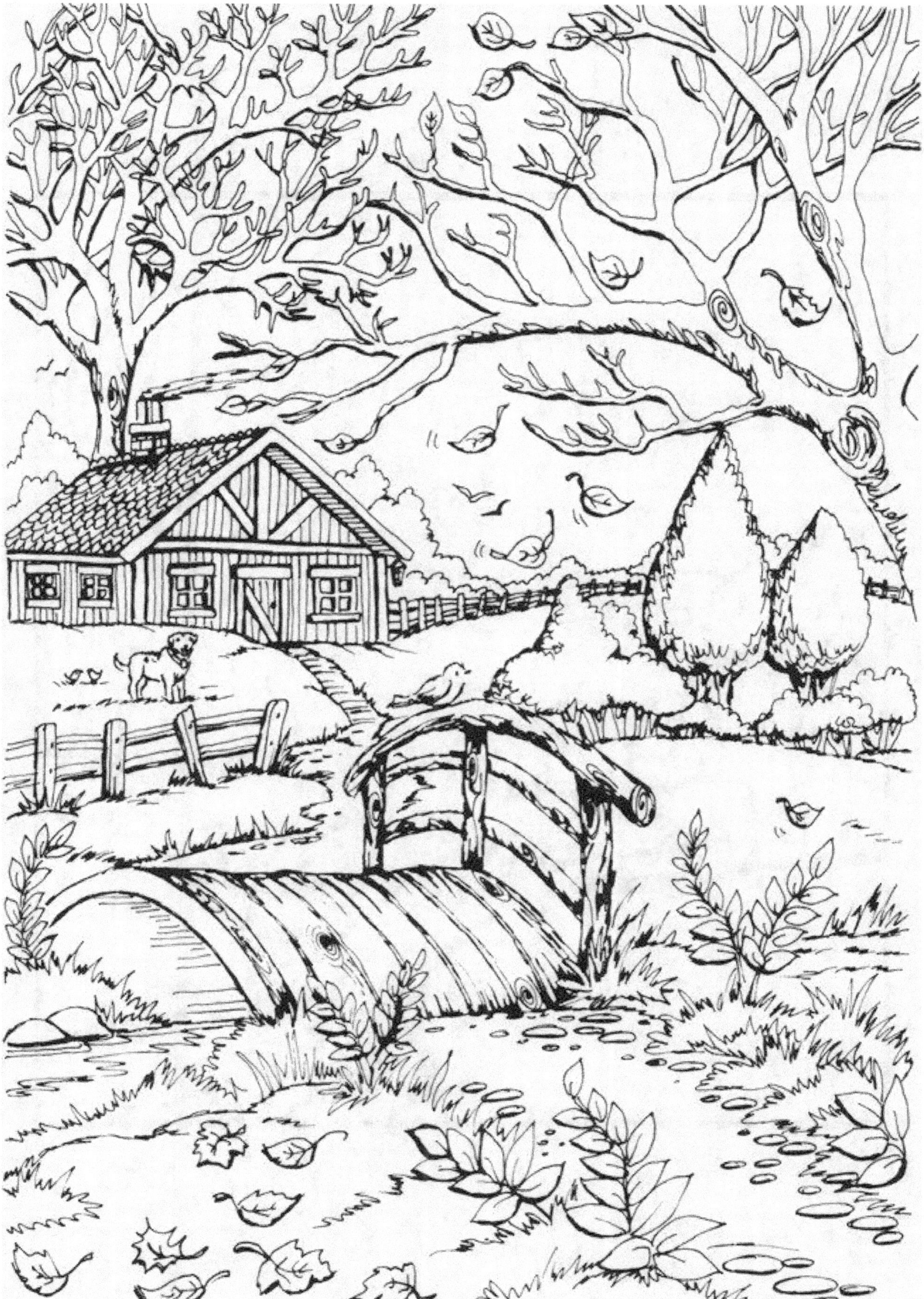

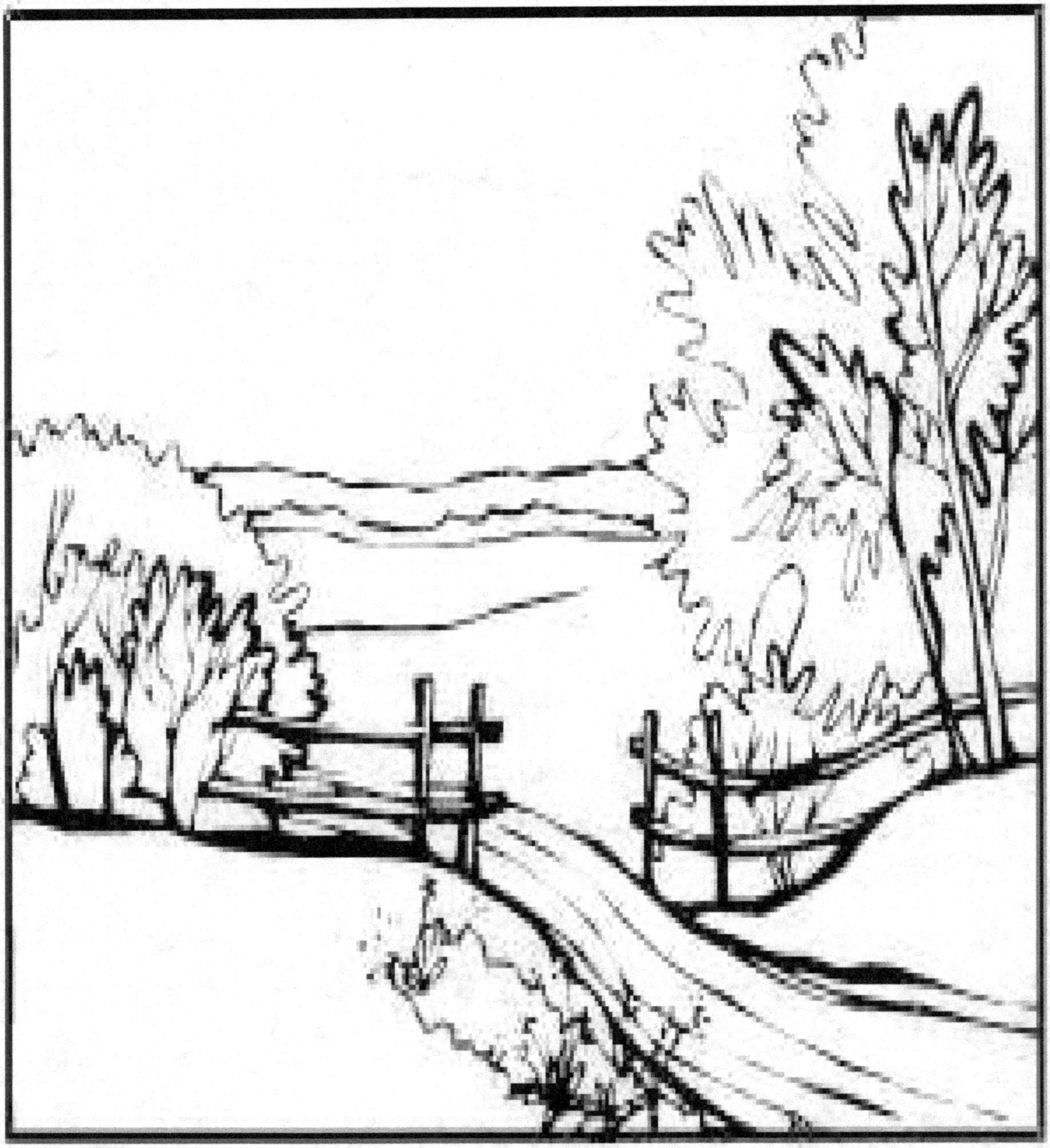

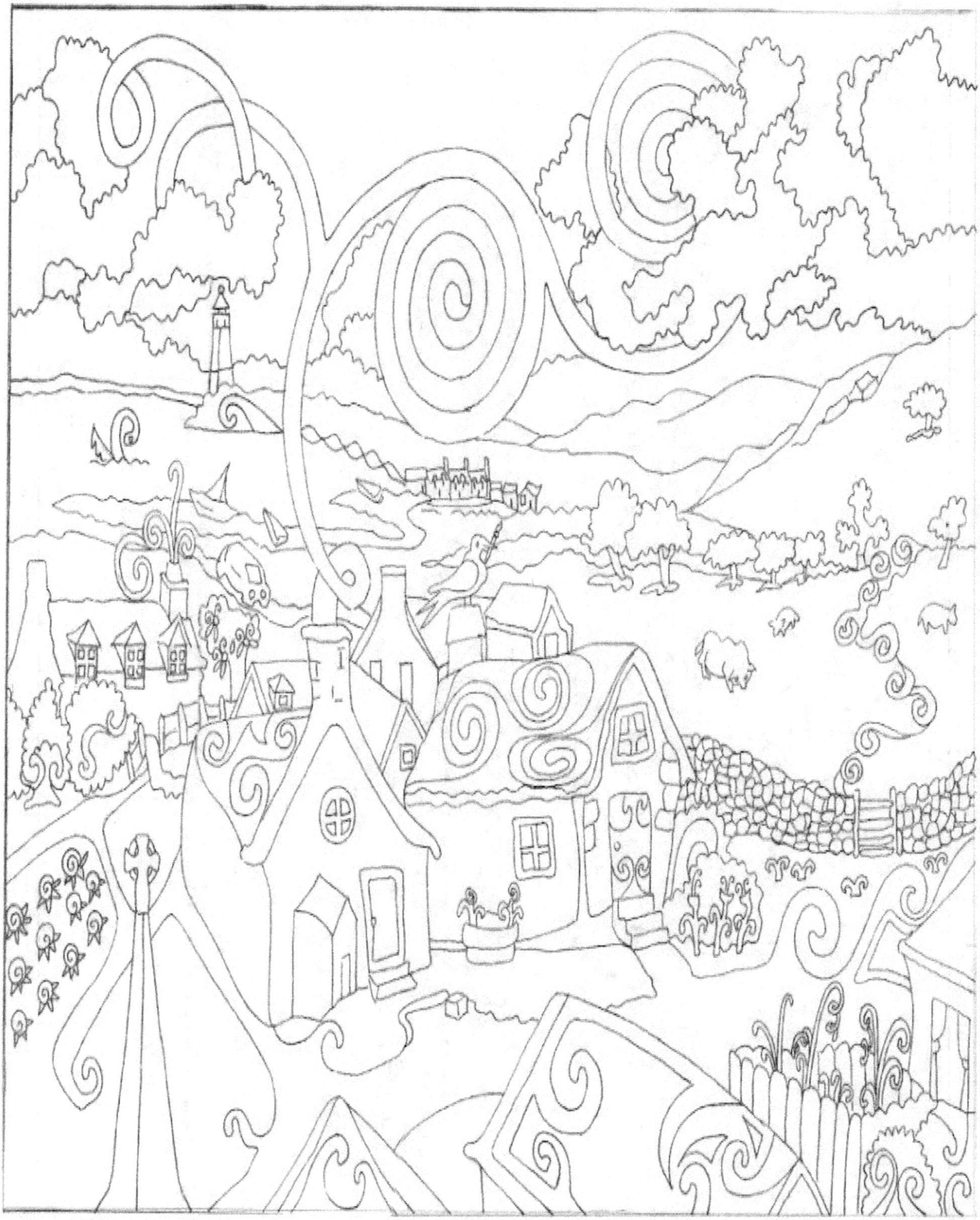

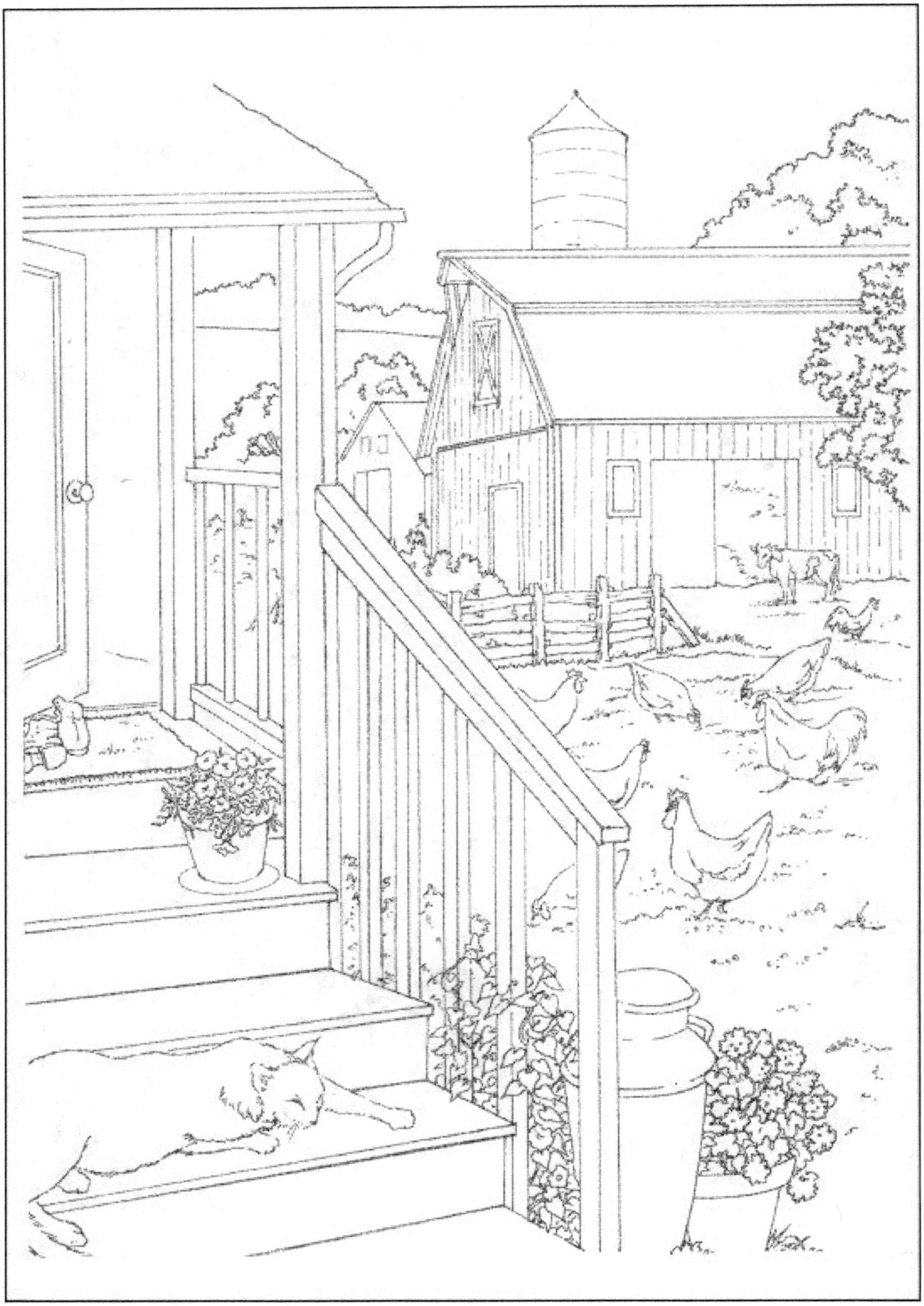

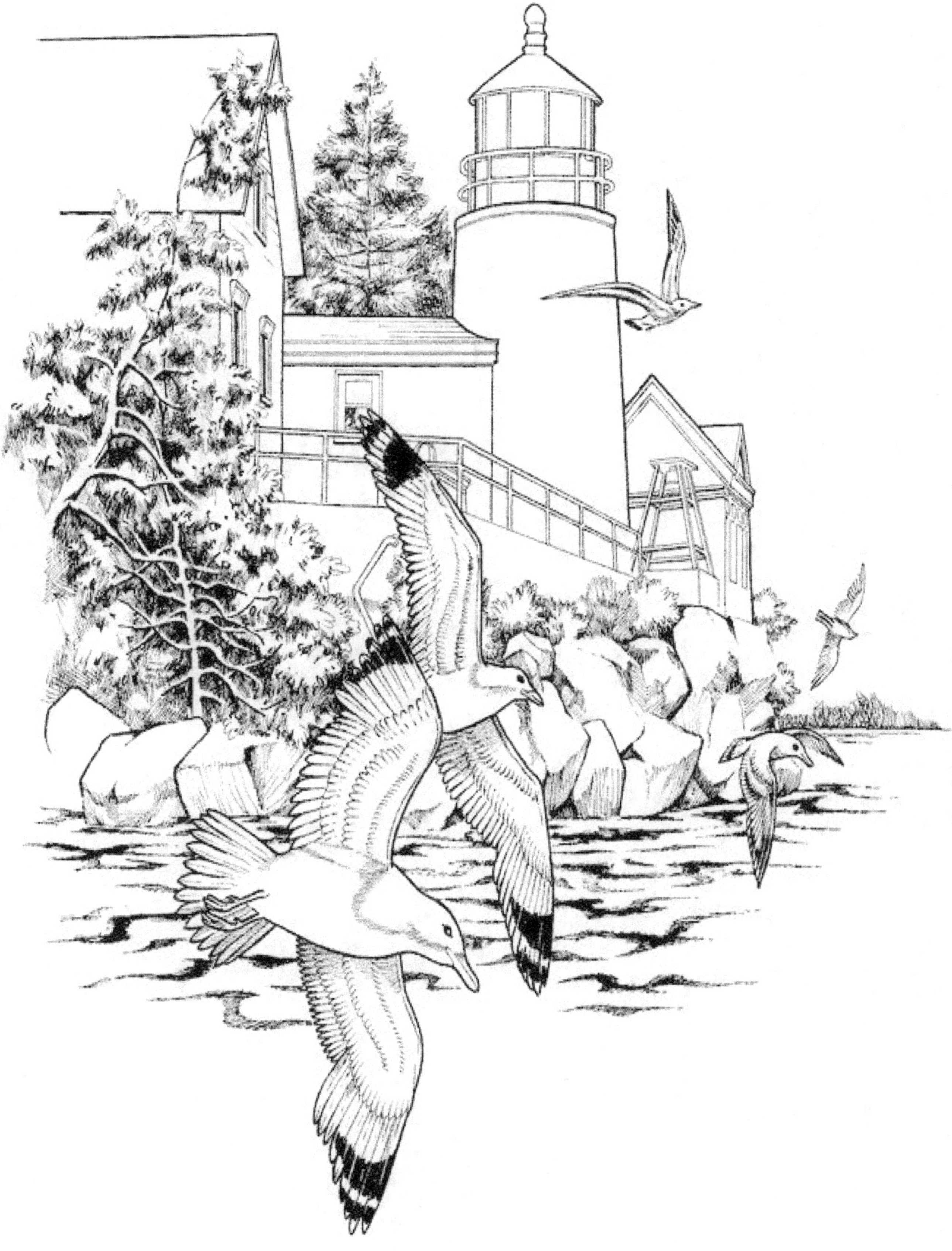

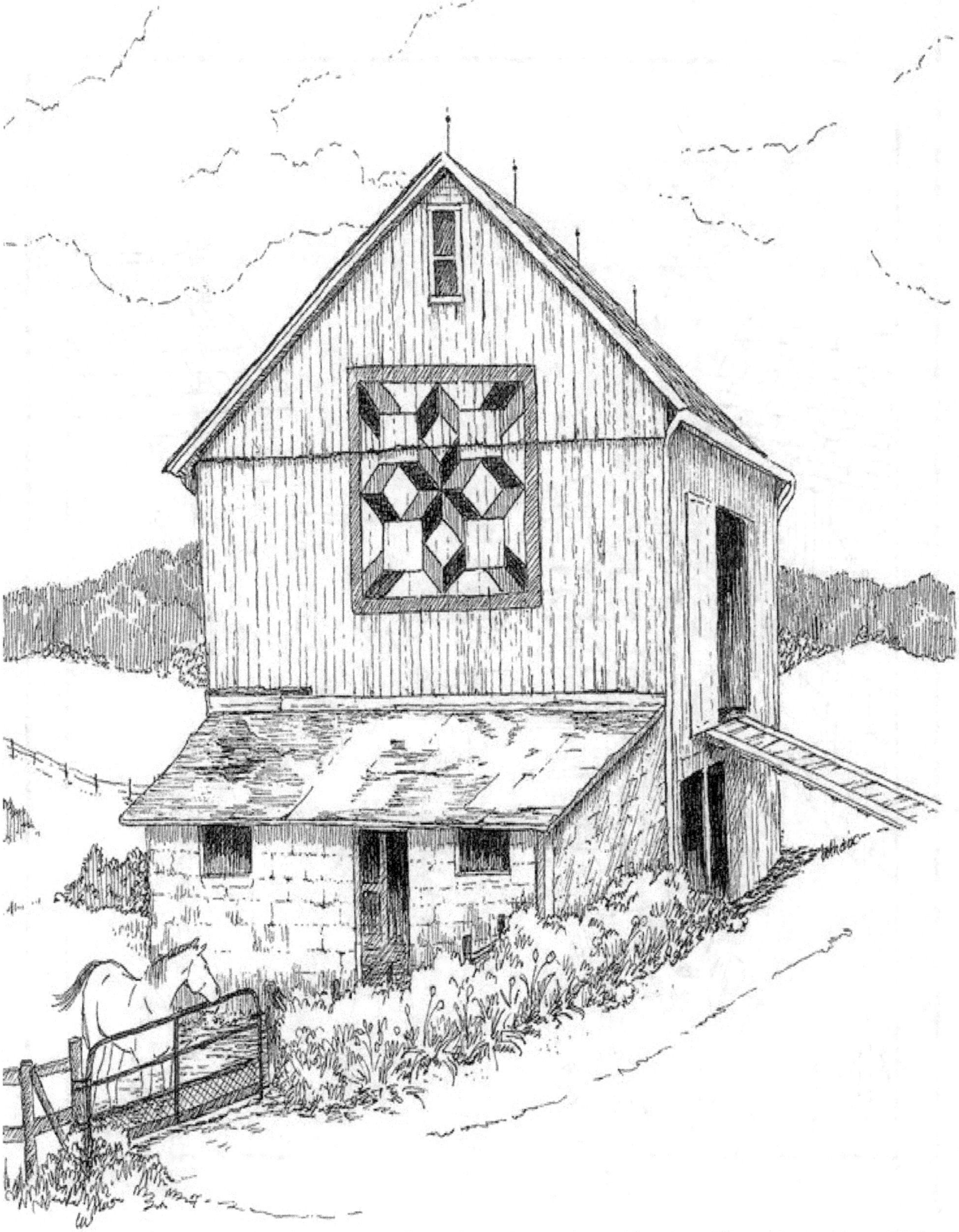

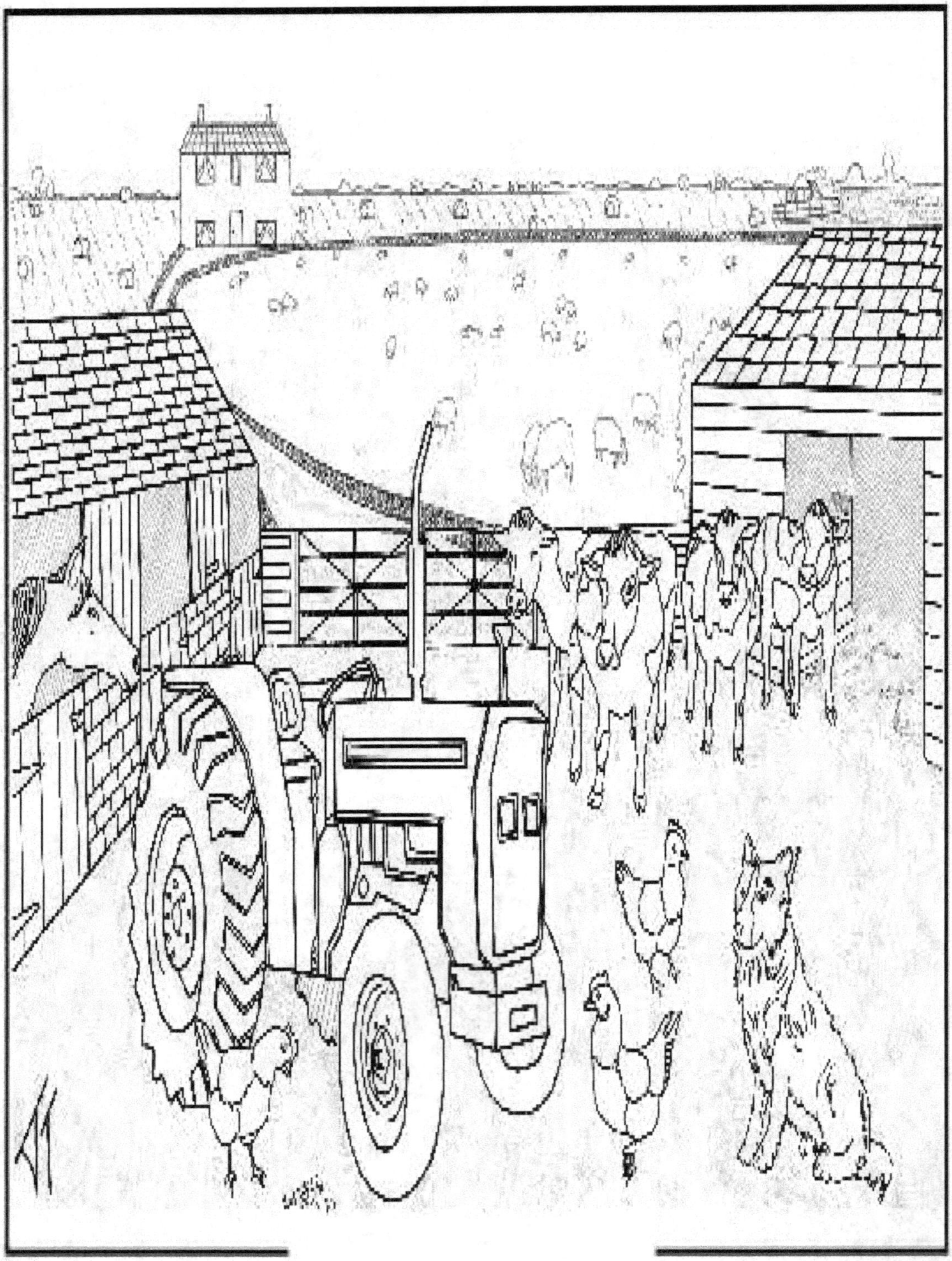

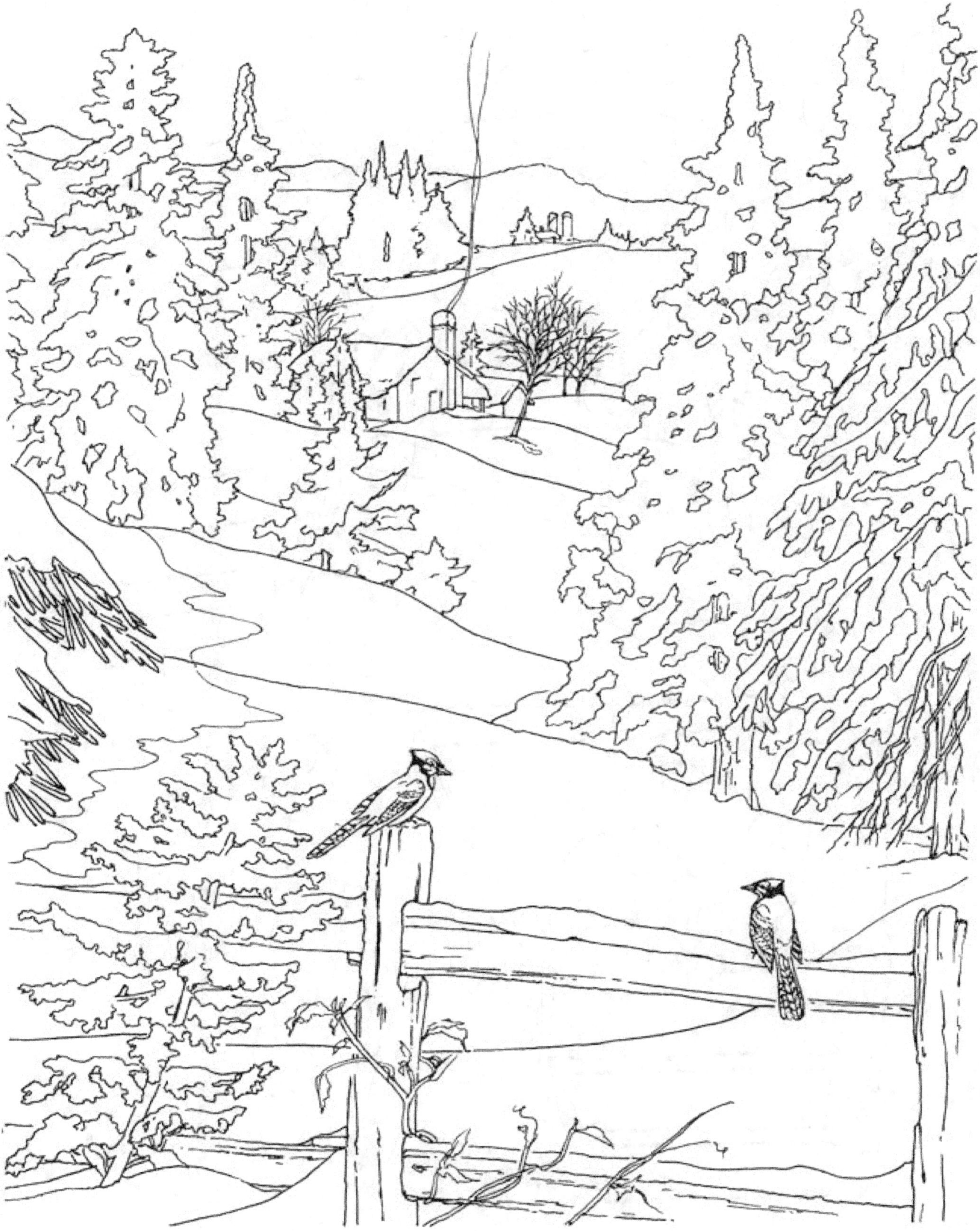

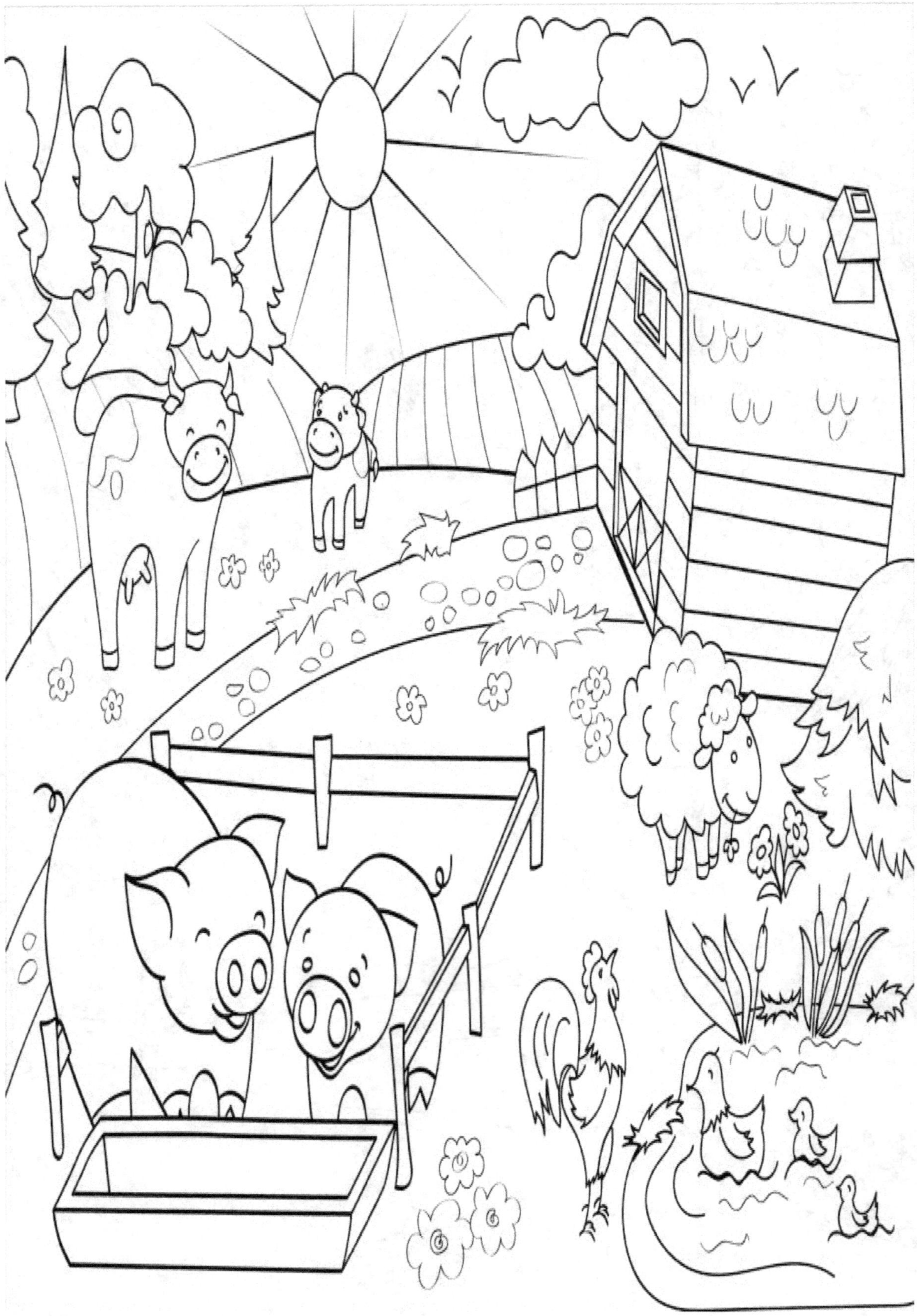

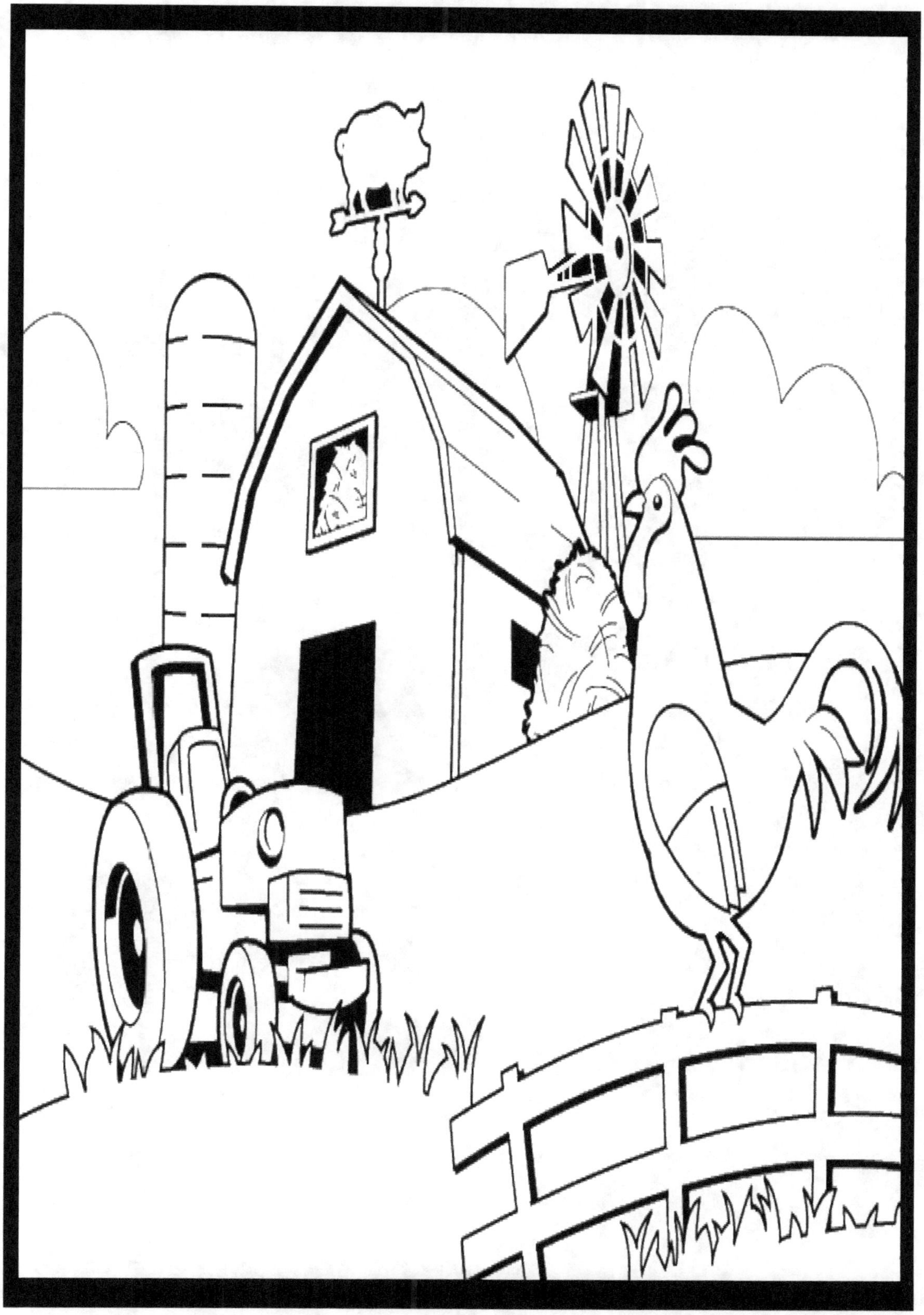

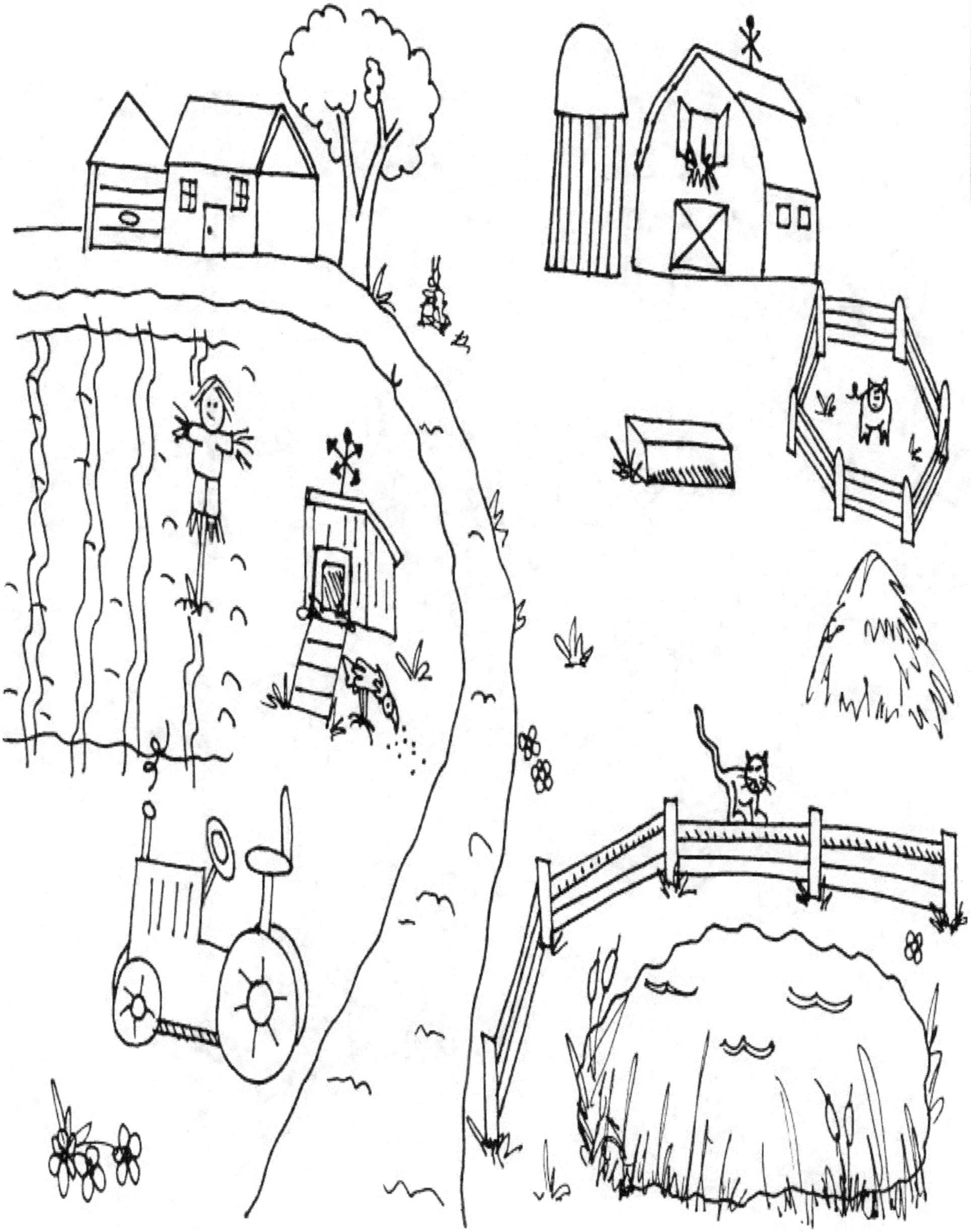

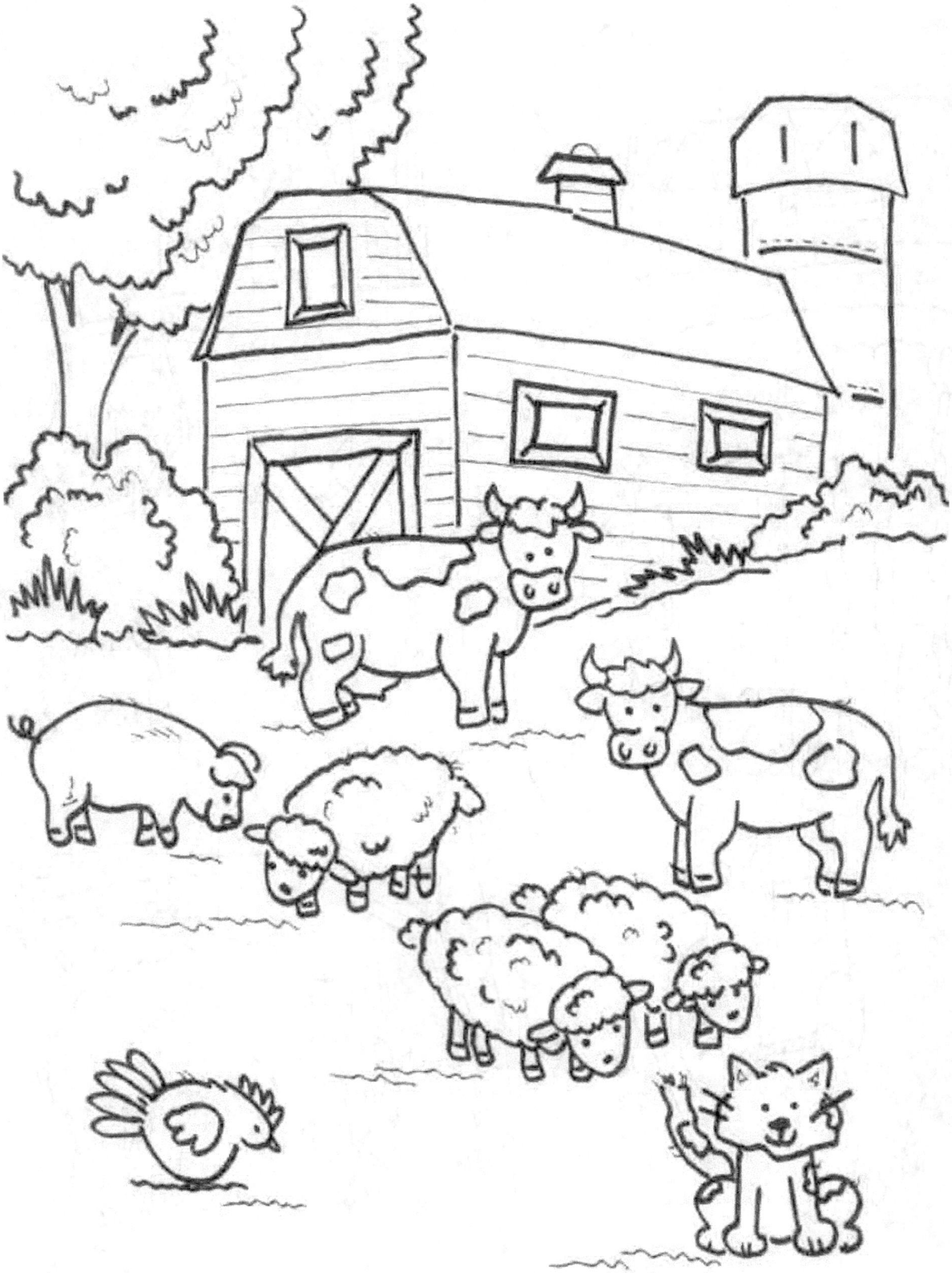

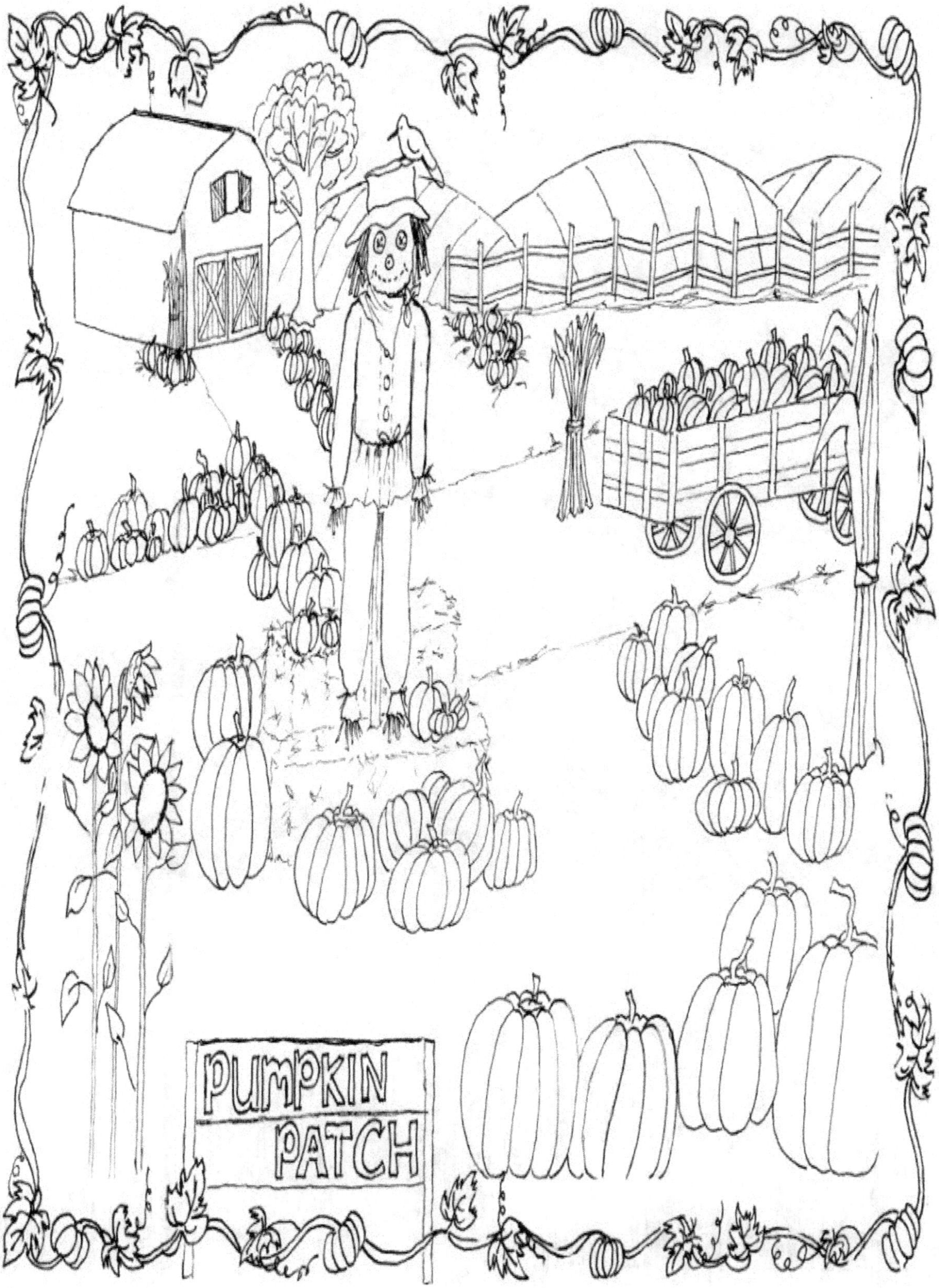
PUMPKIN
PATCH

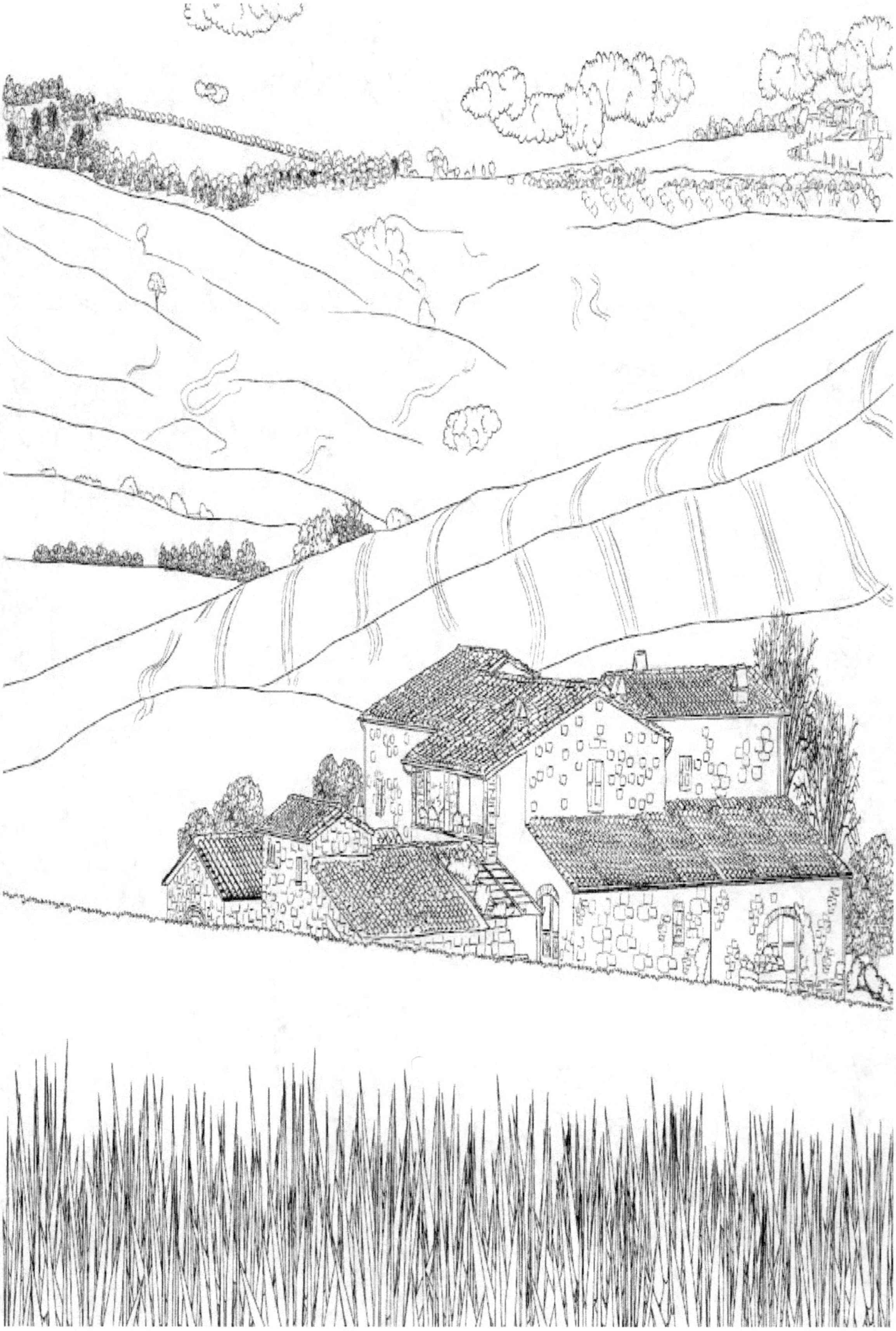

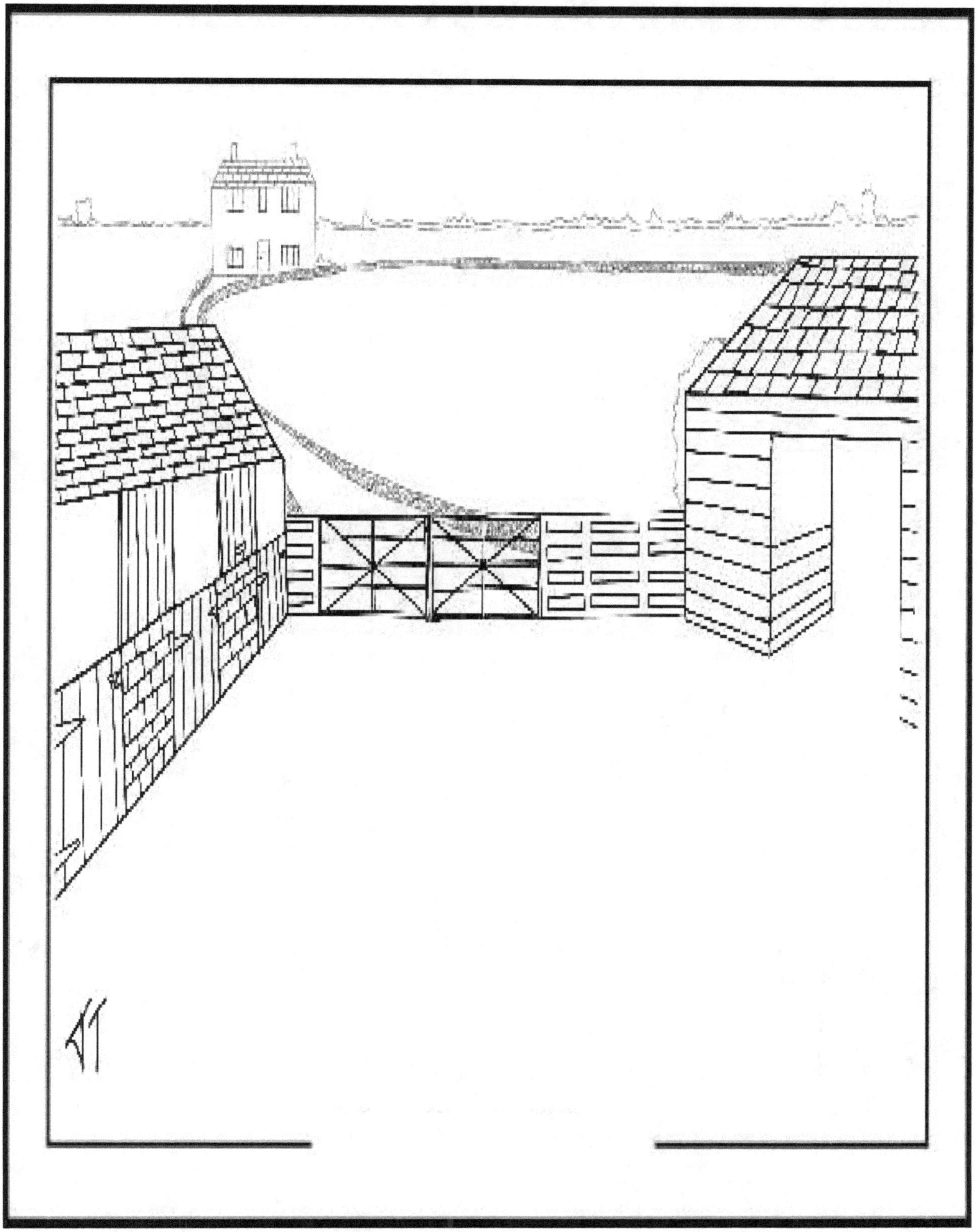

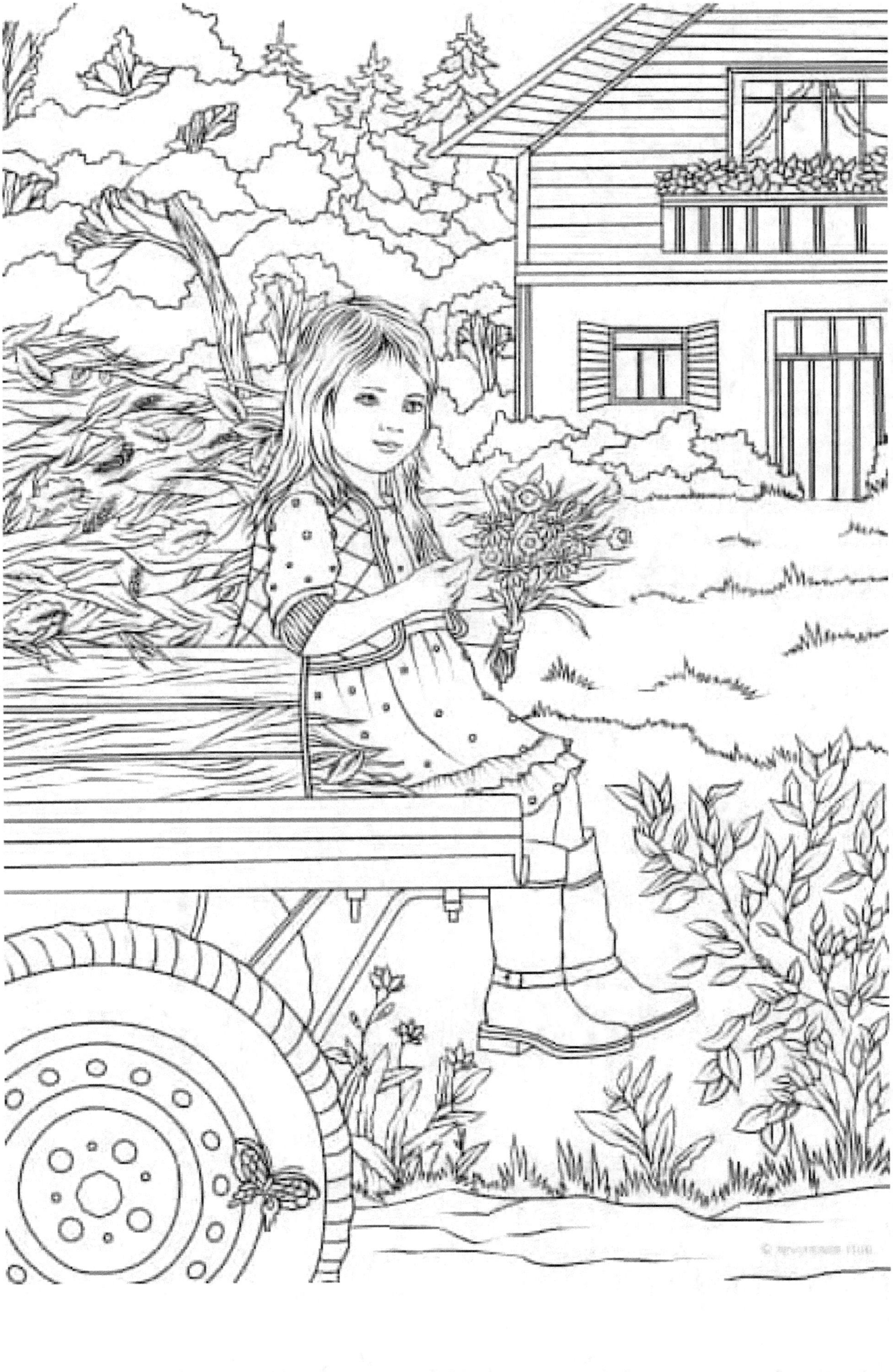

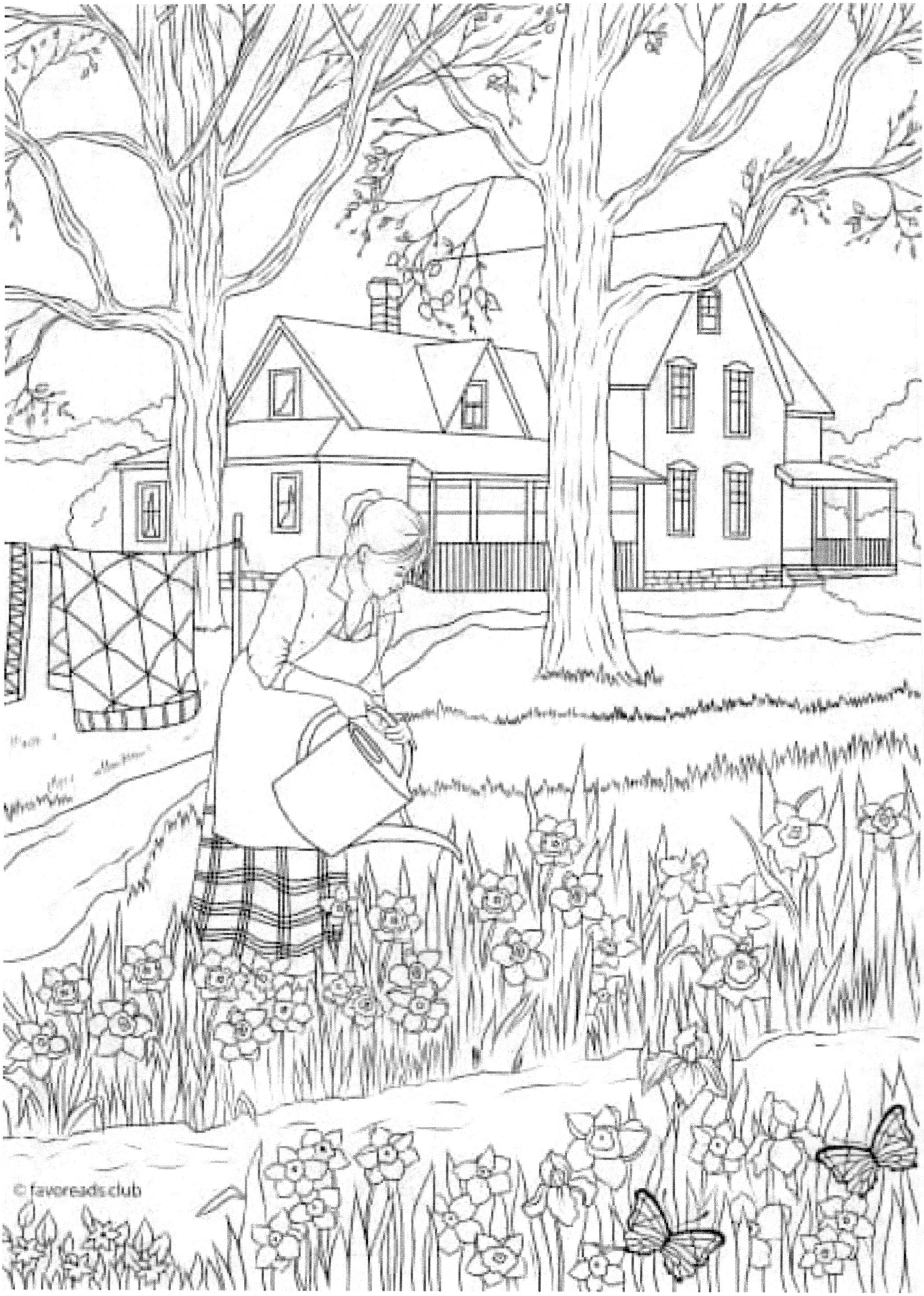
© favoreads.club

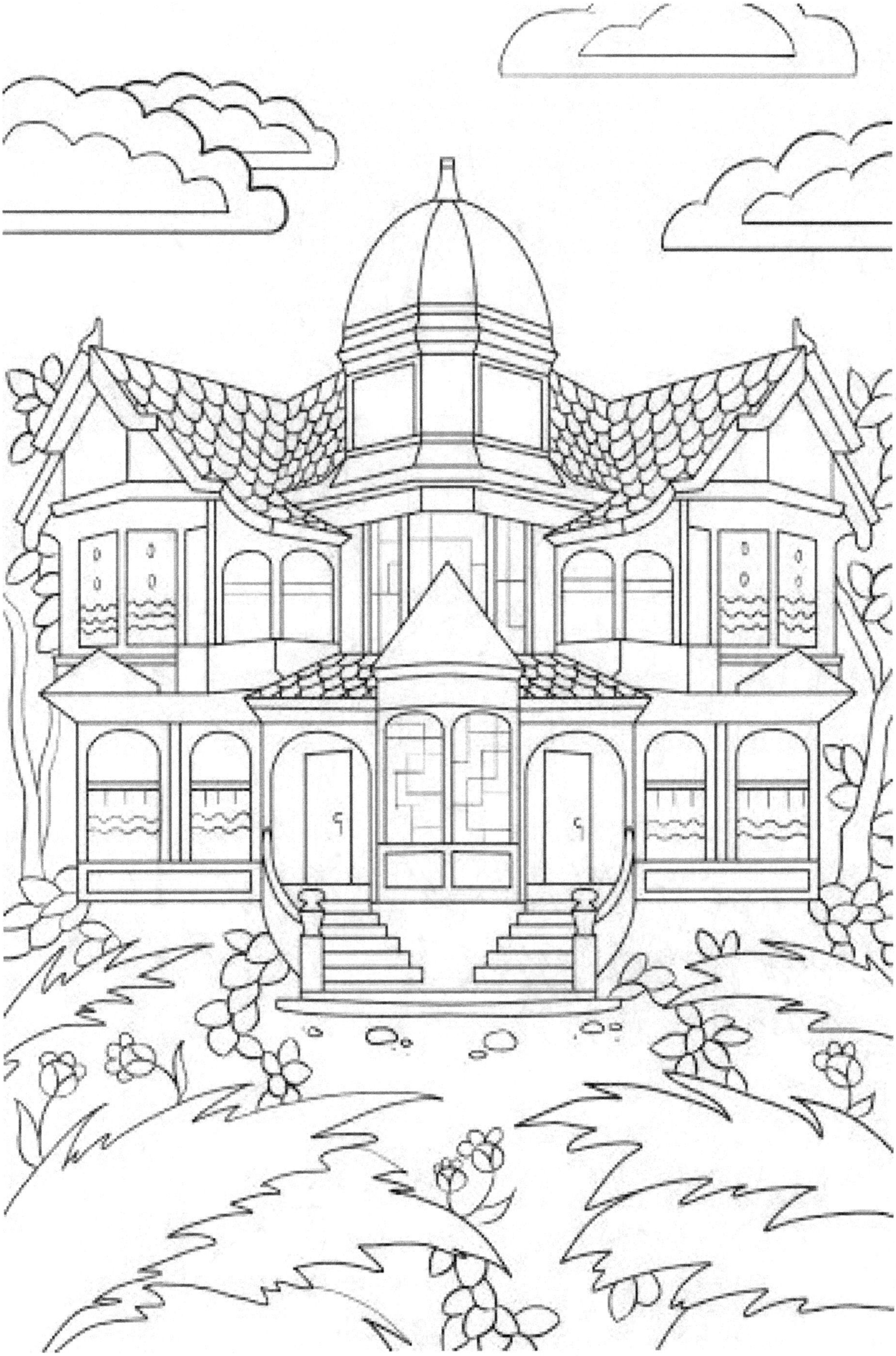

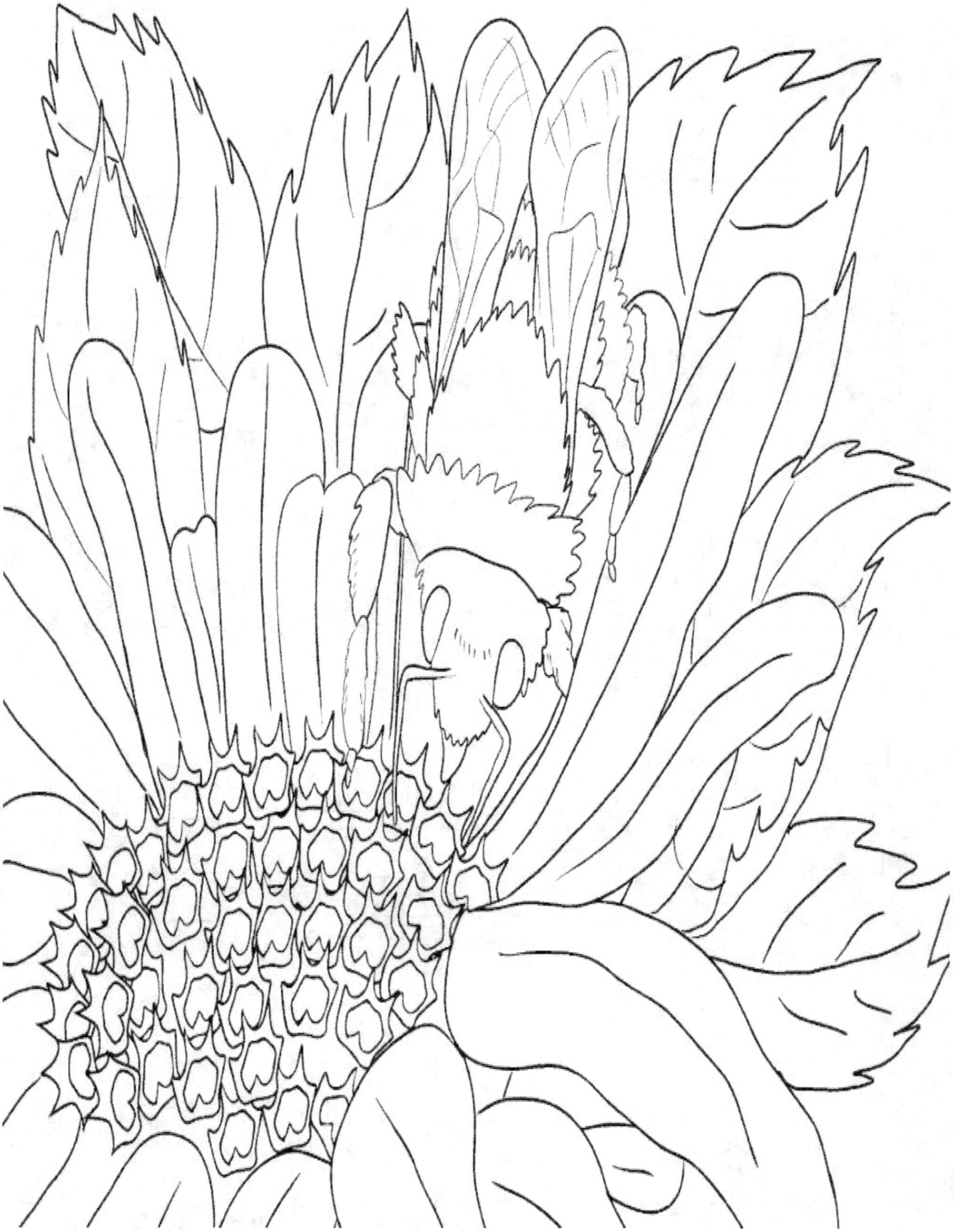

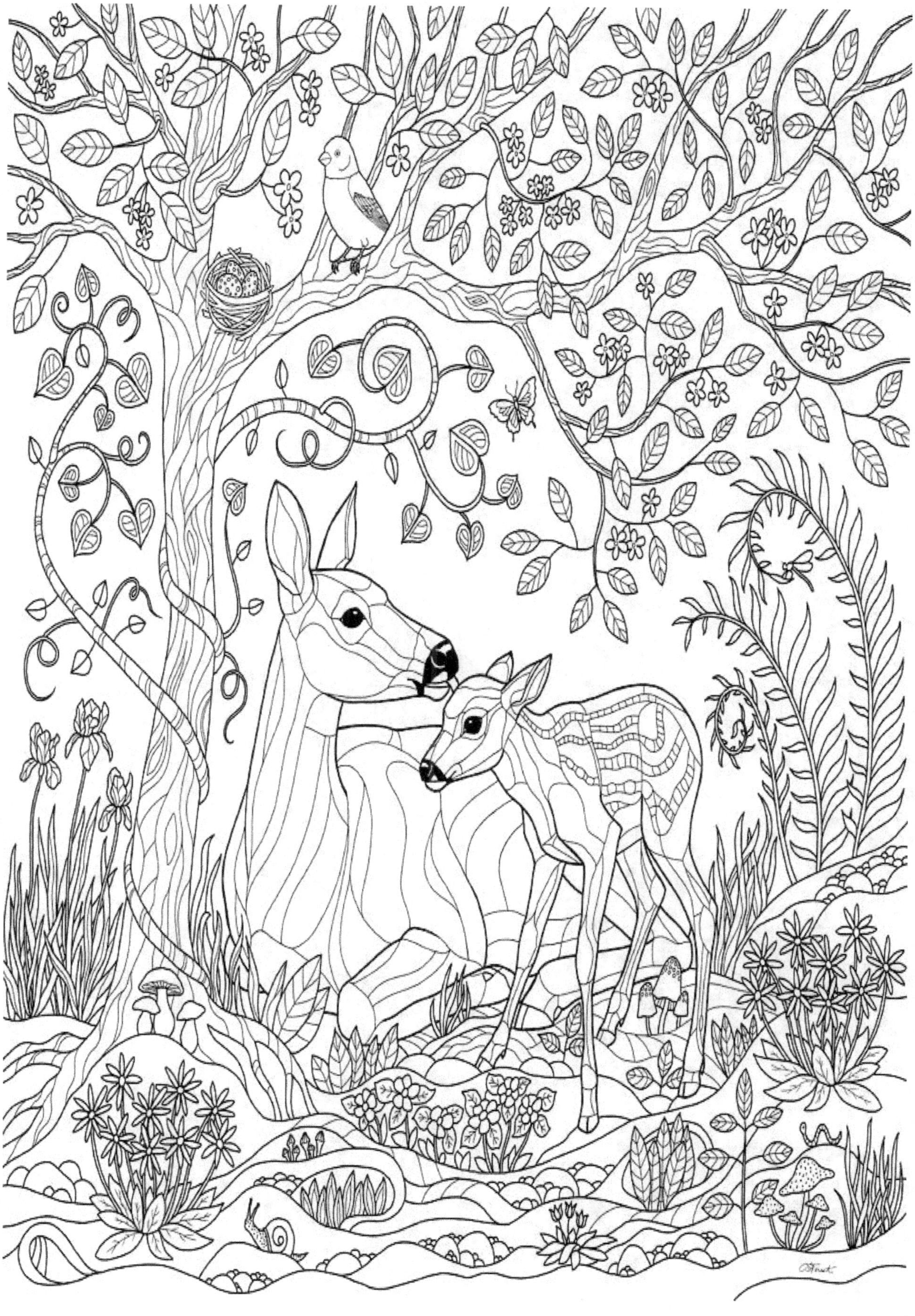

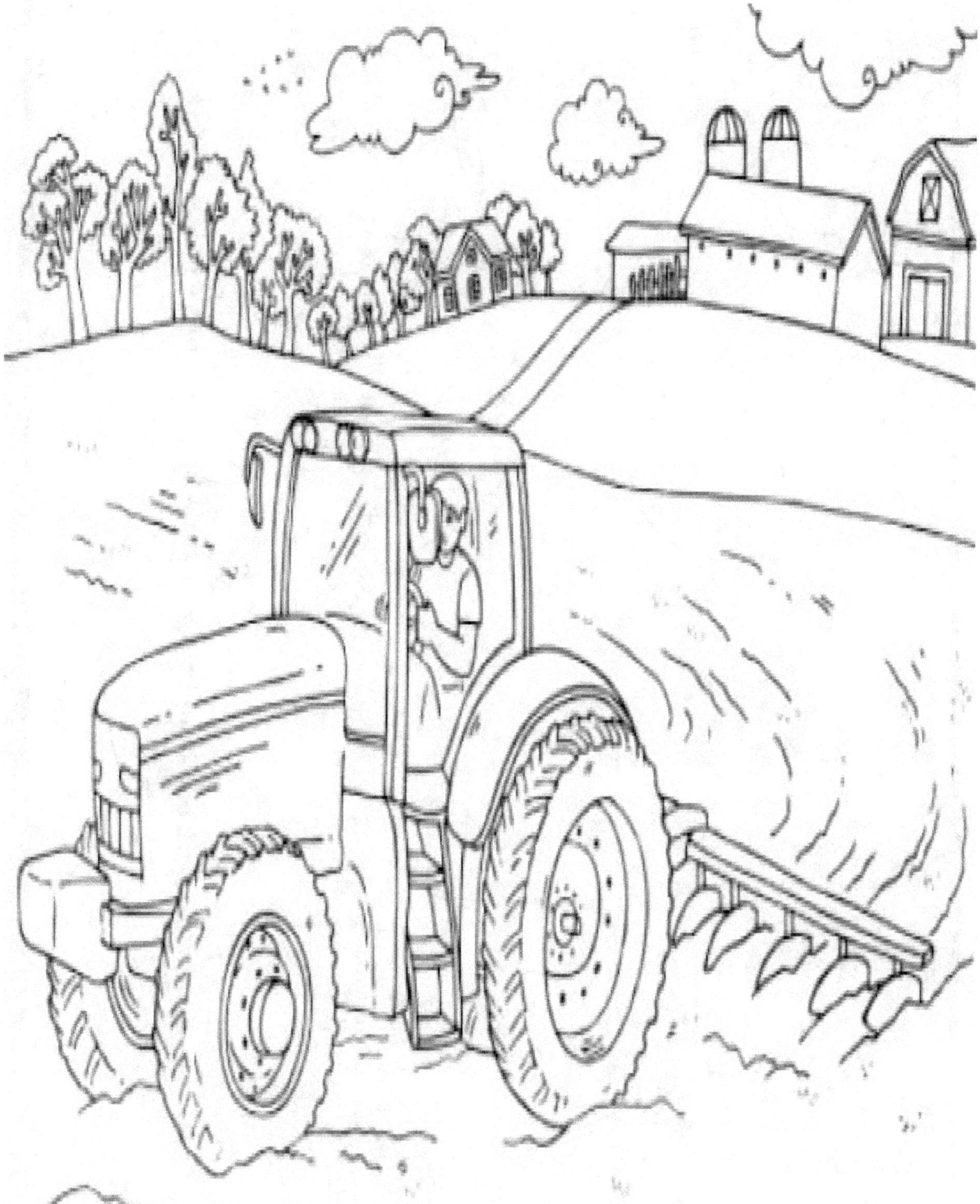

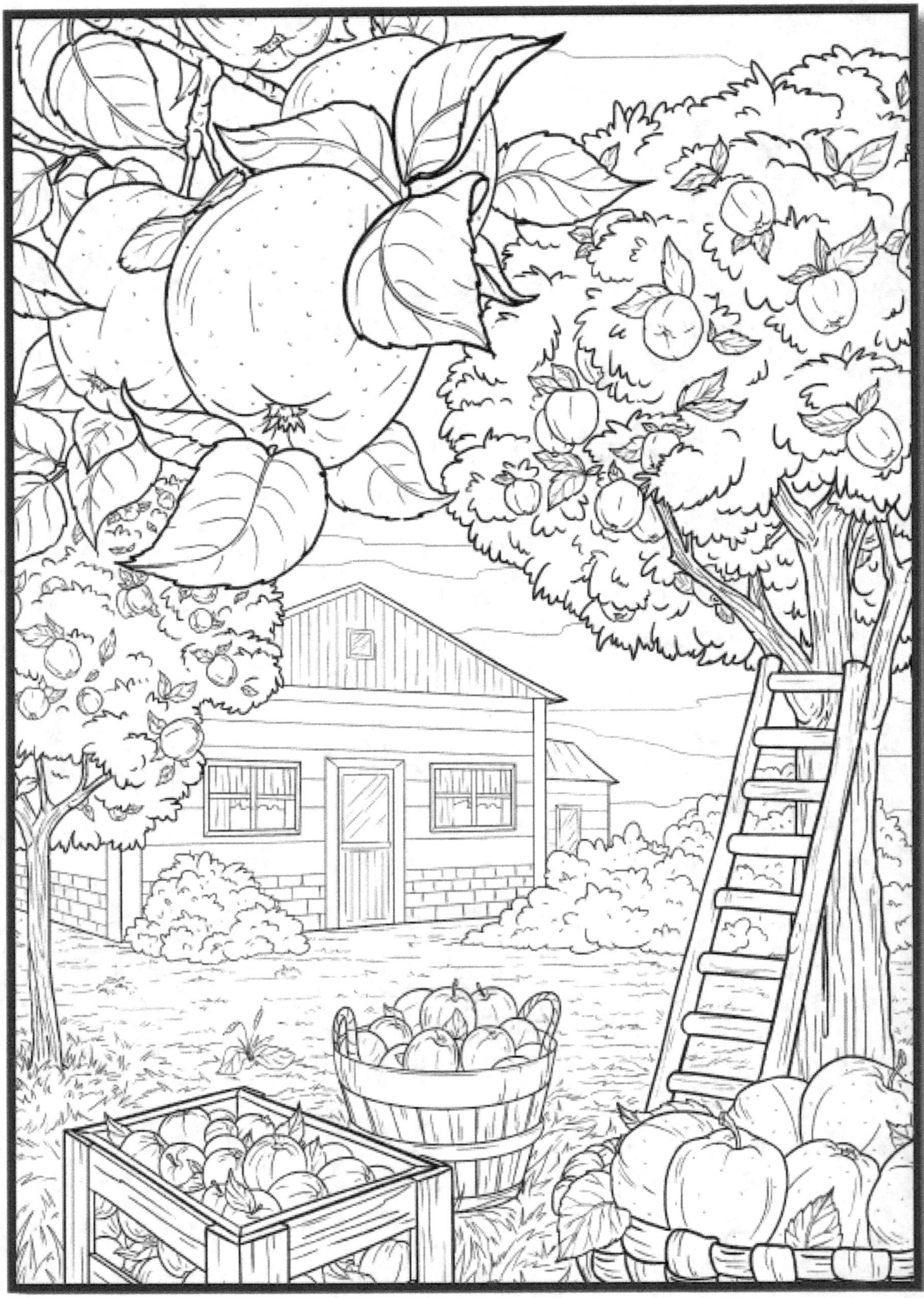

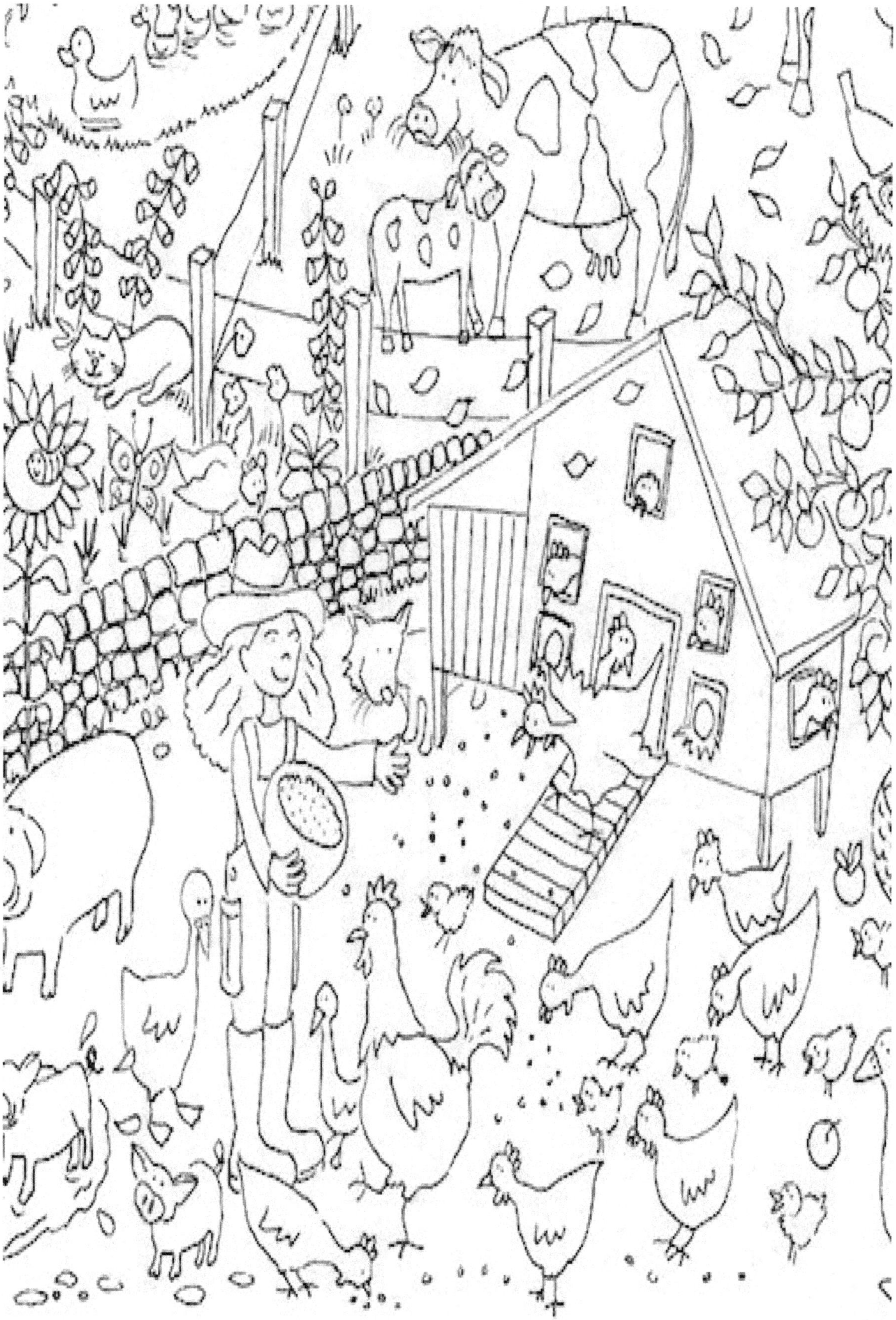

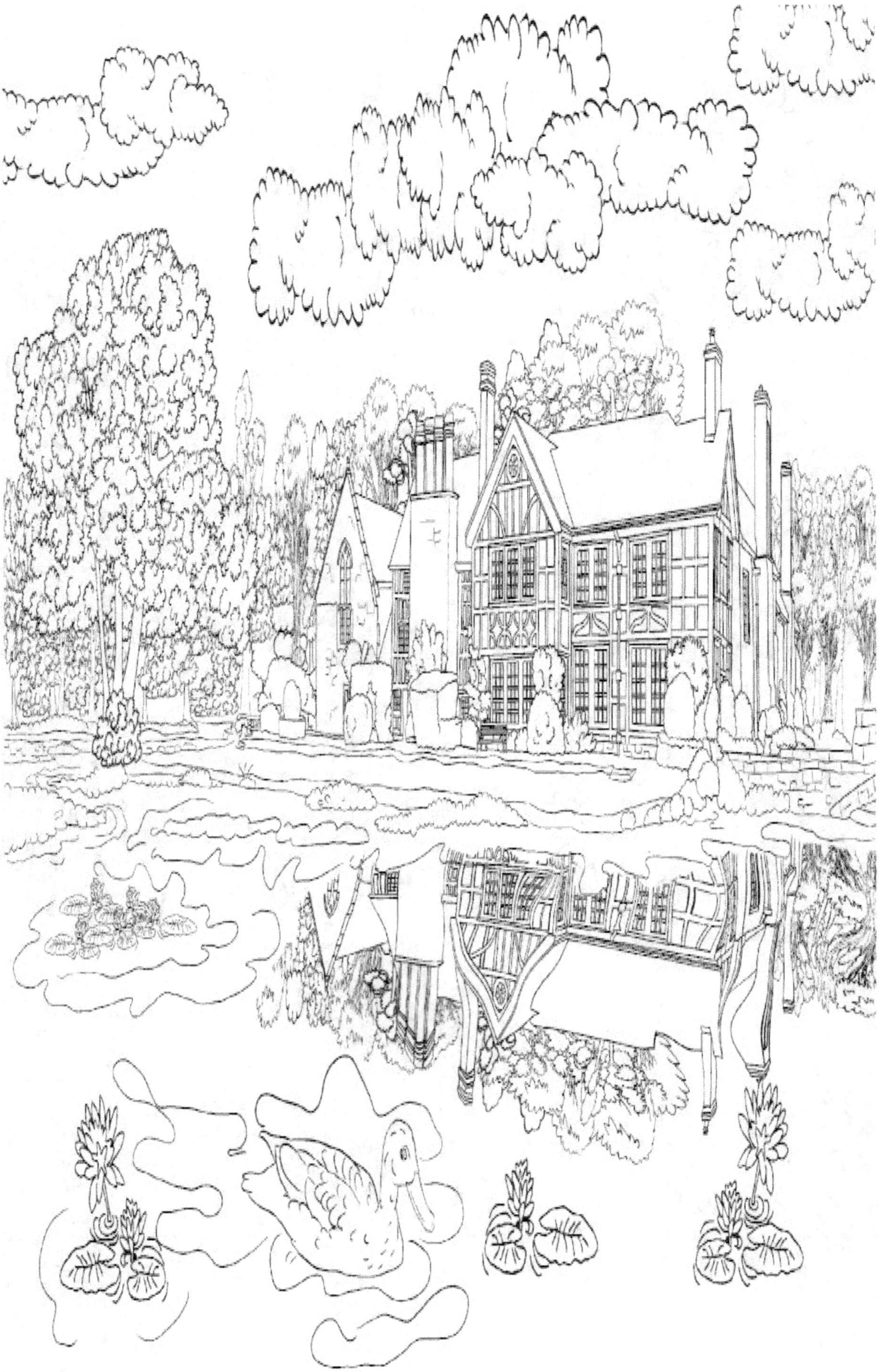

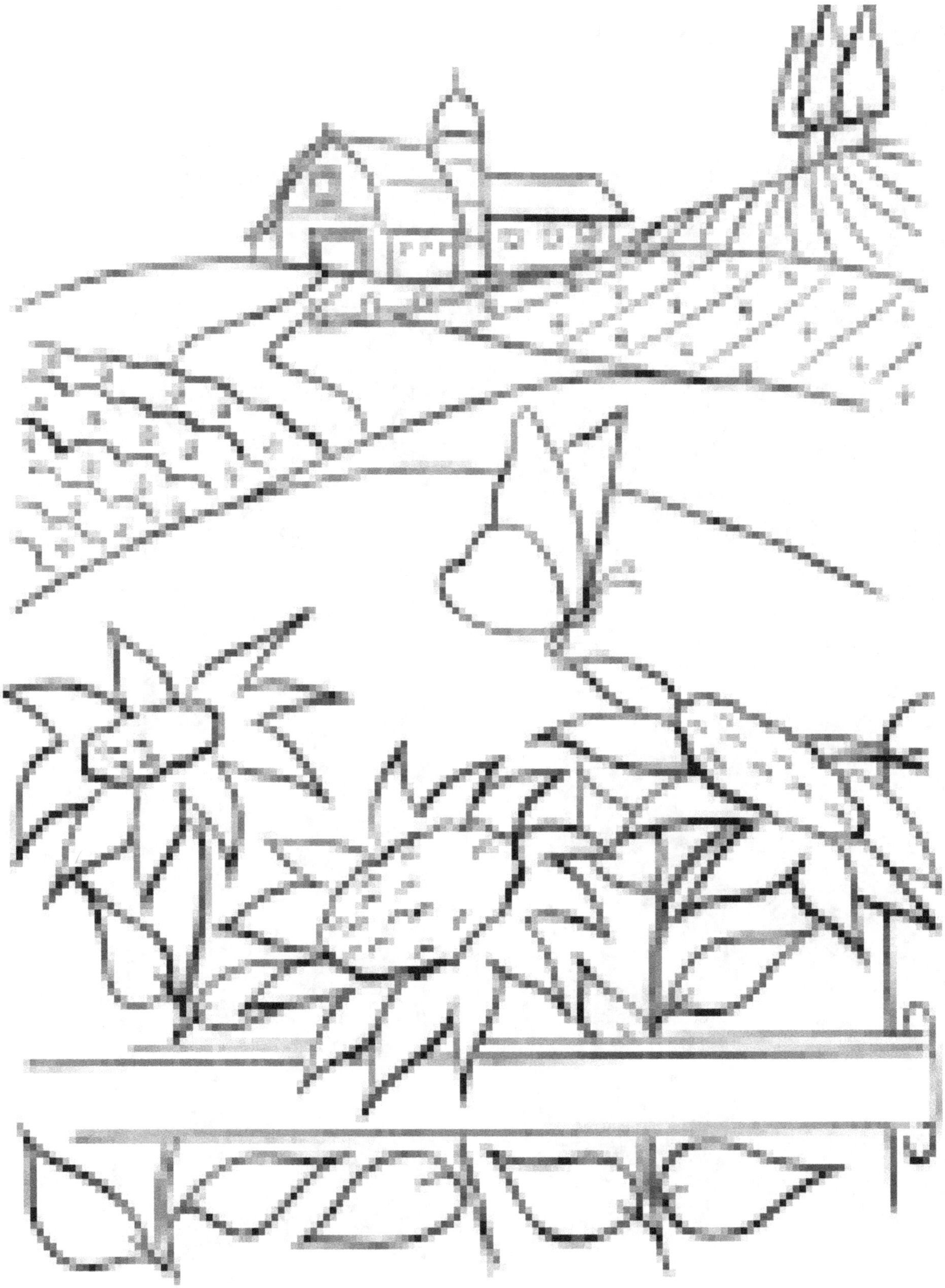

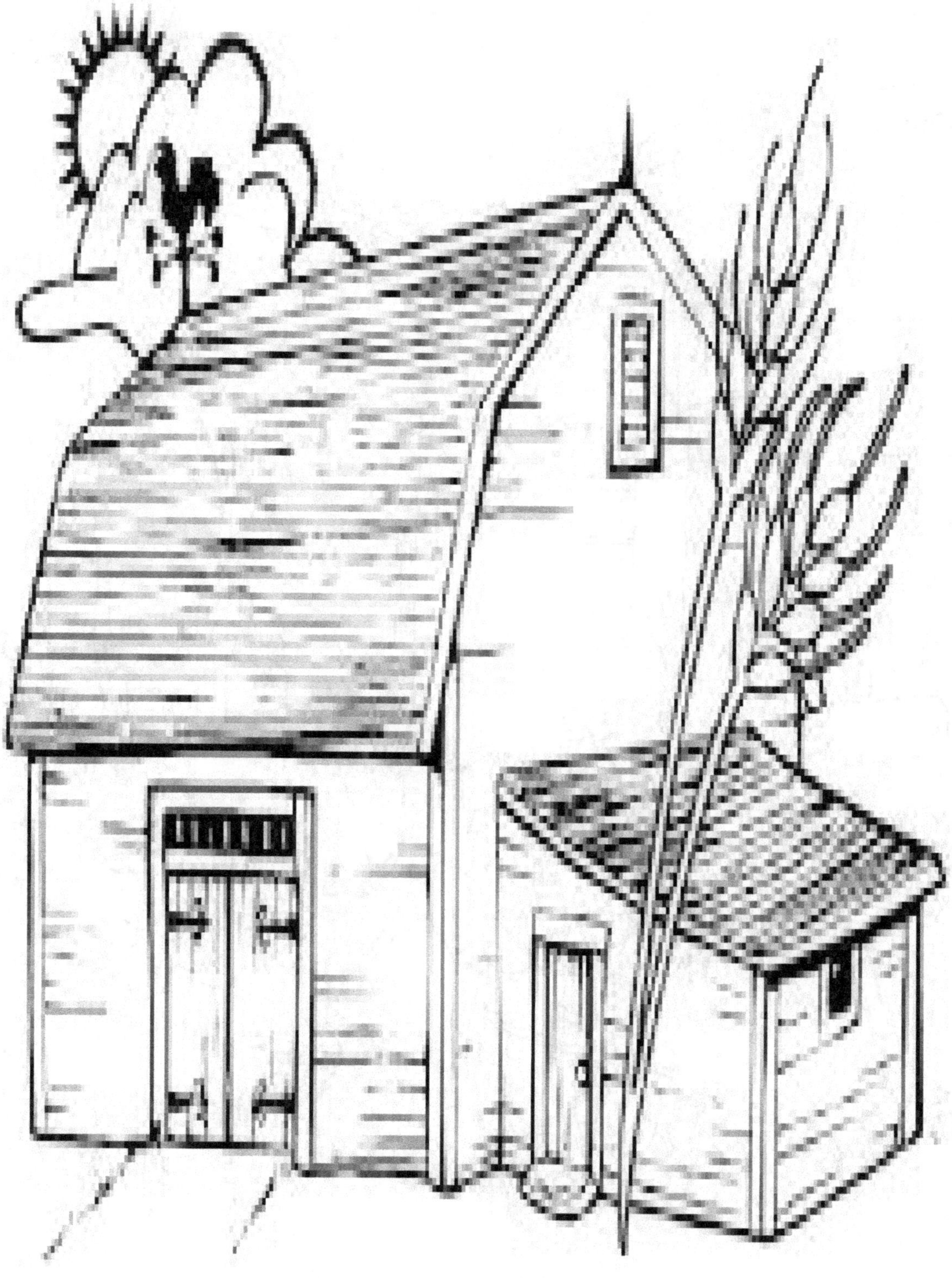

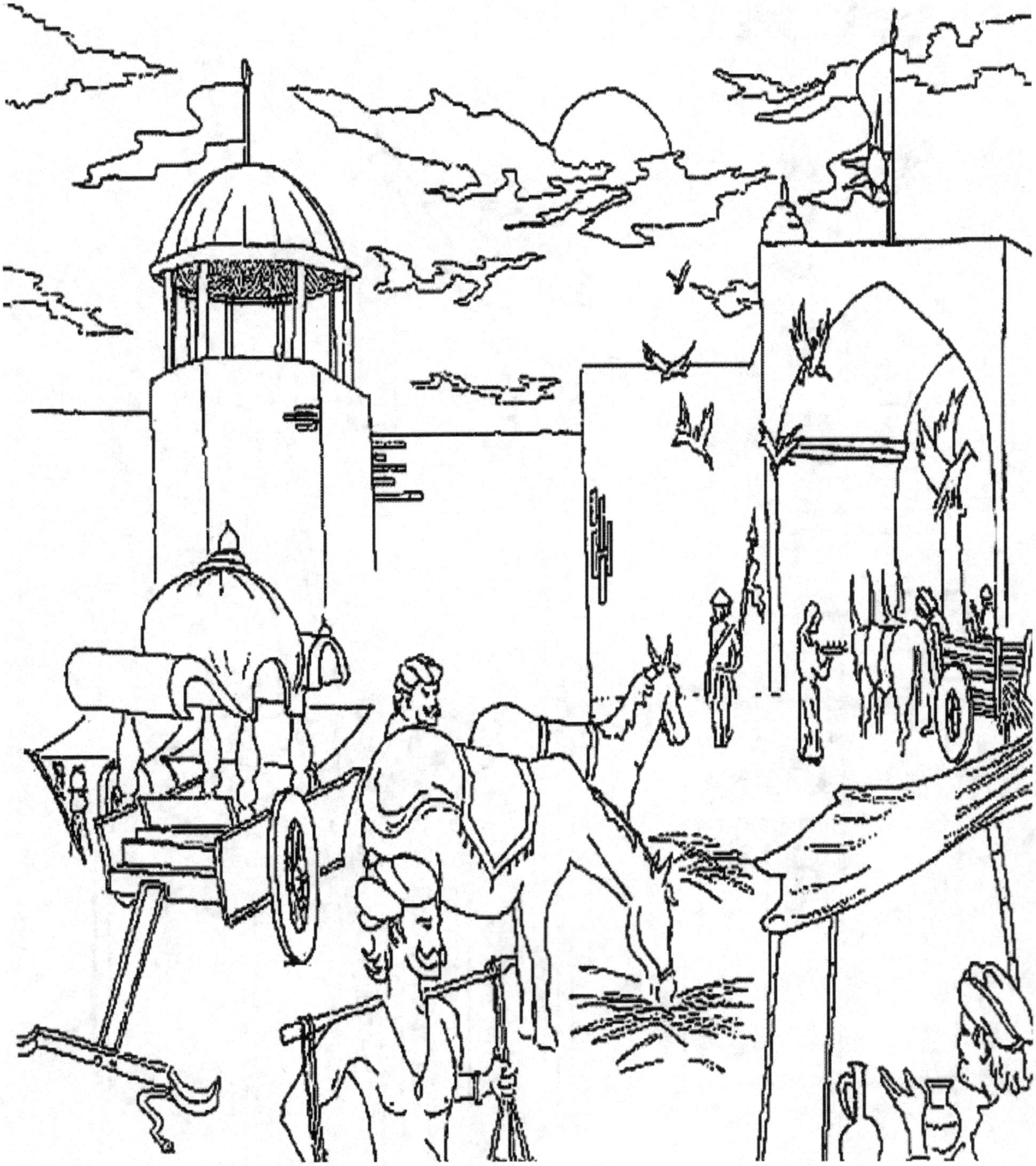

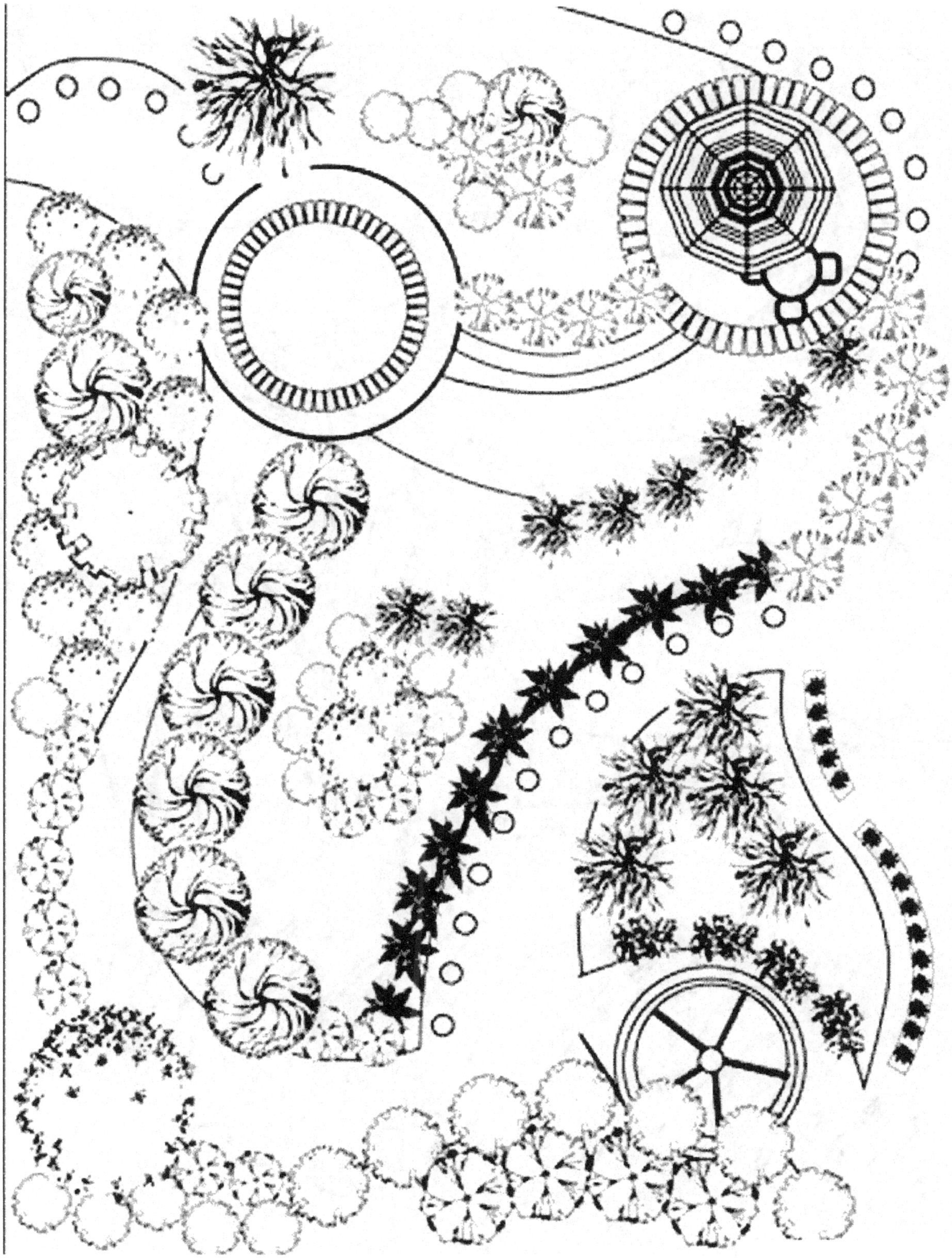

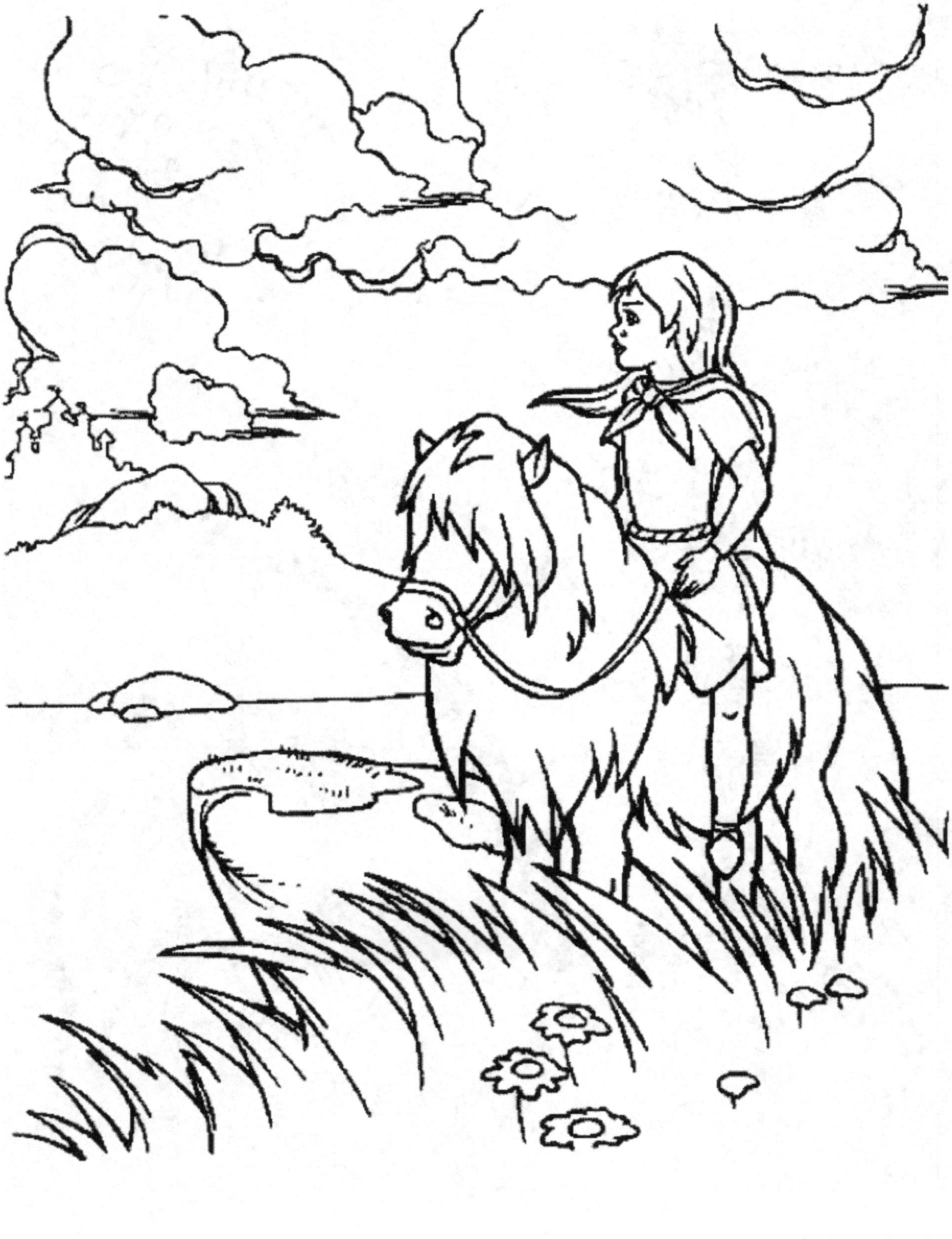

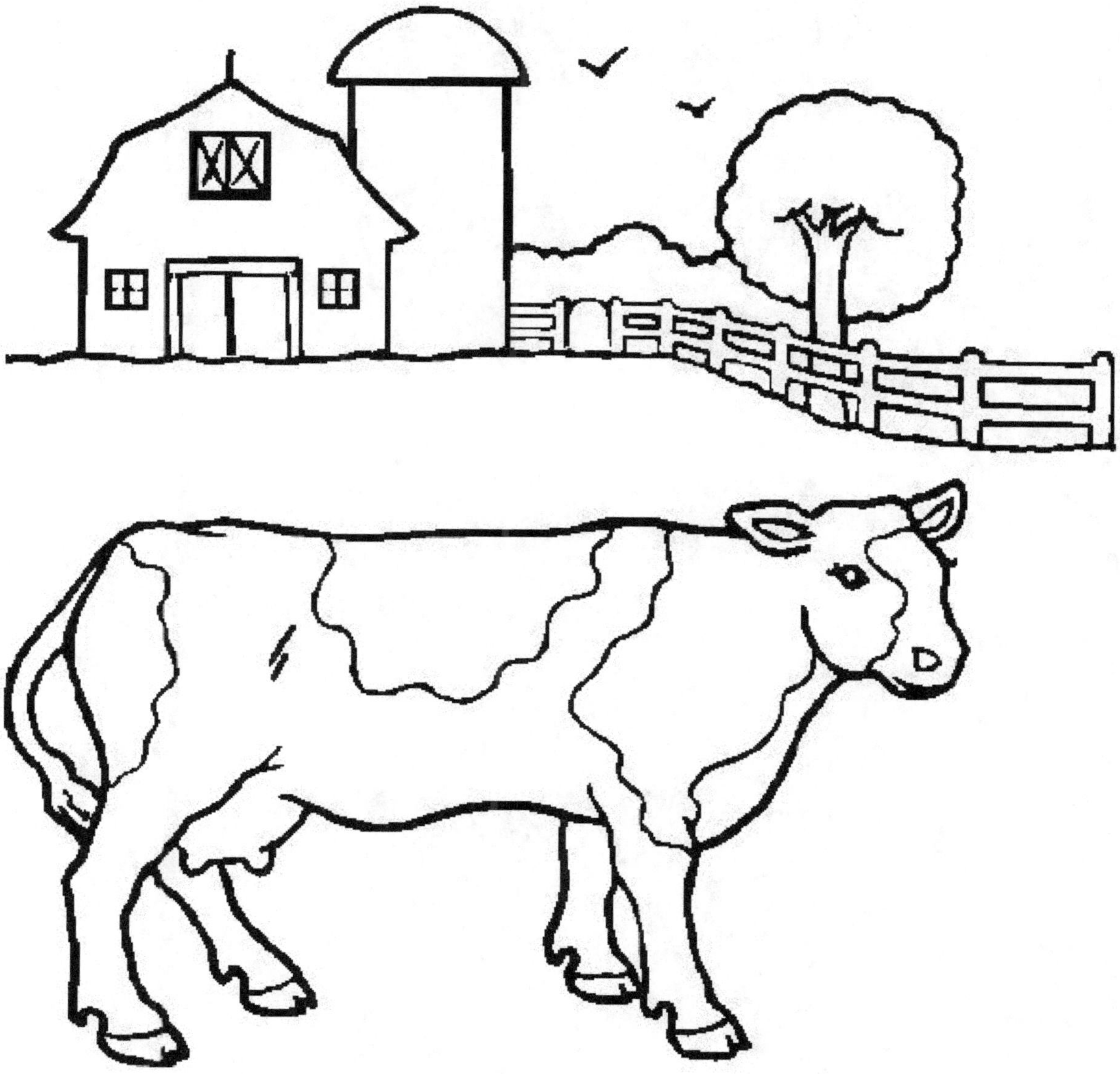

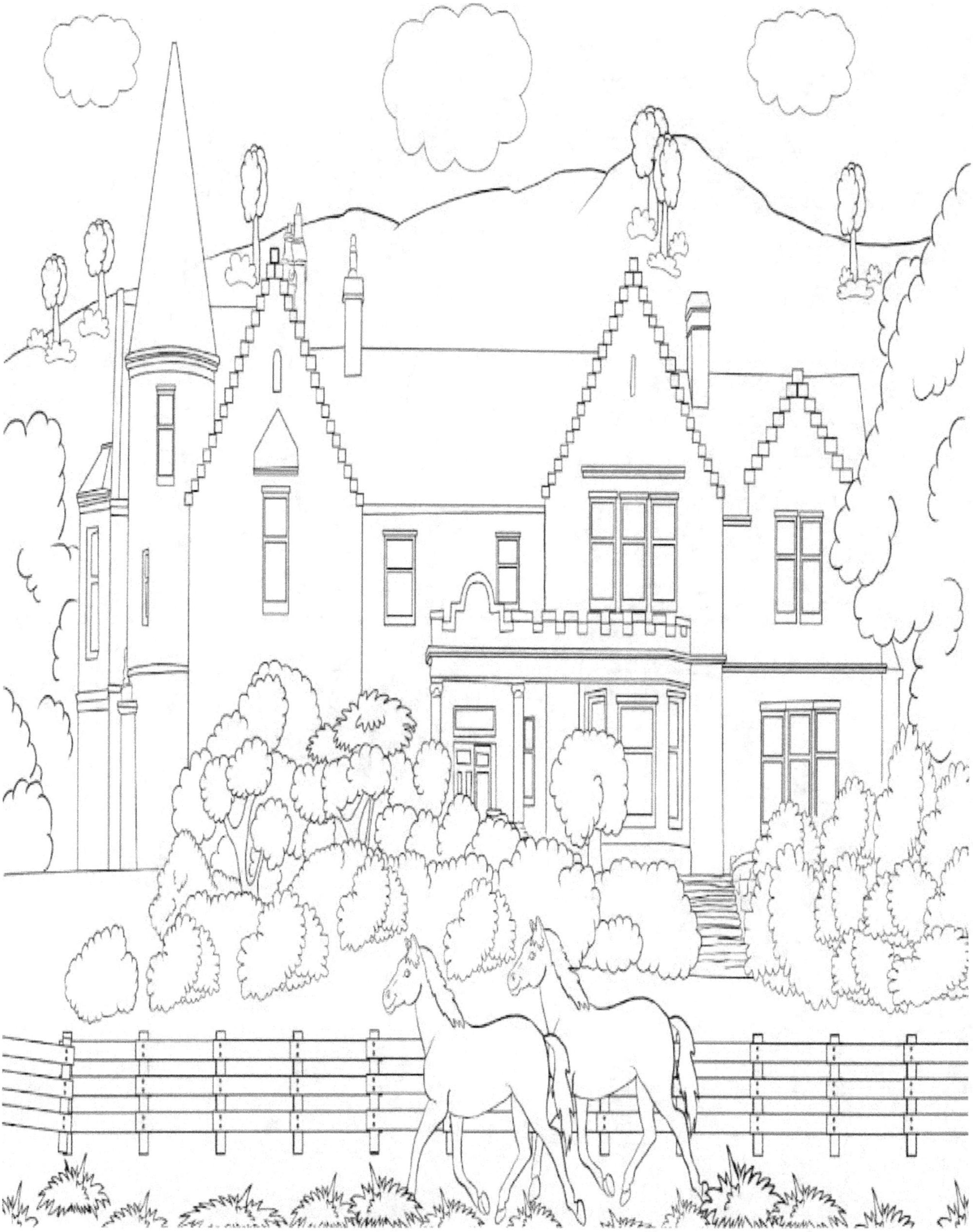

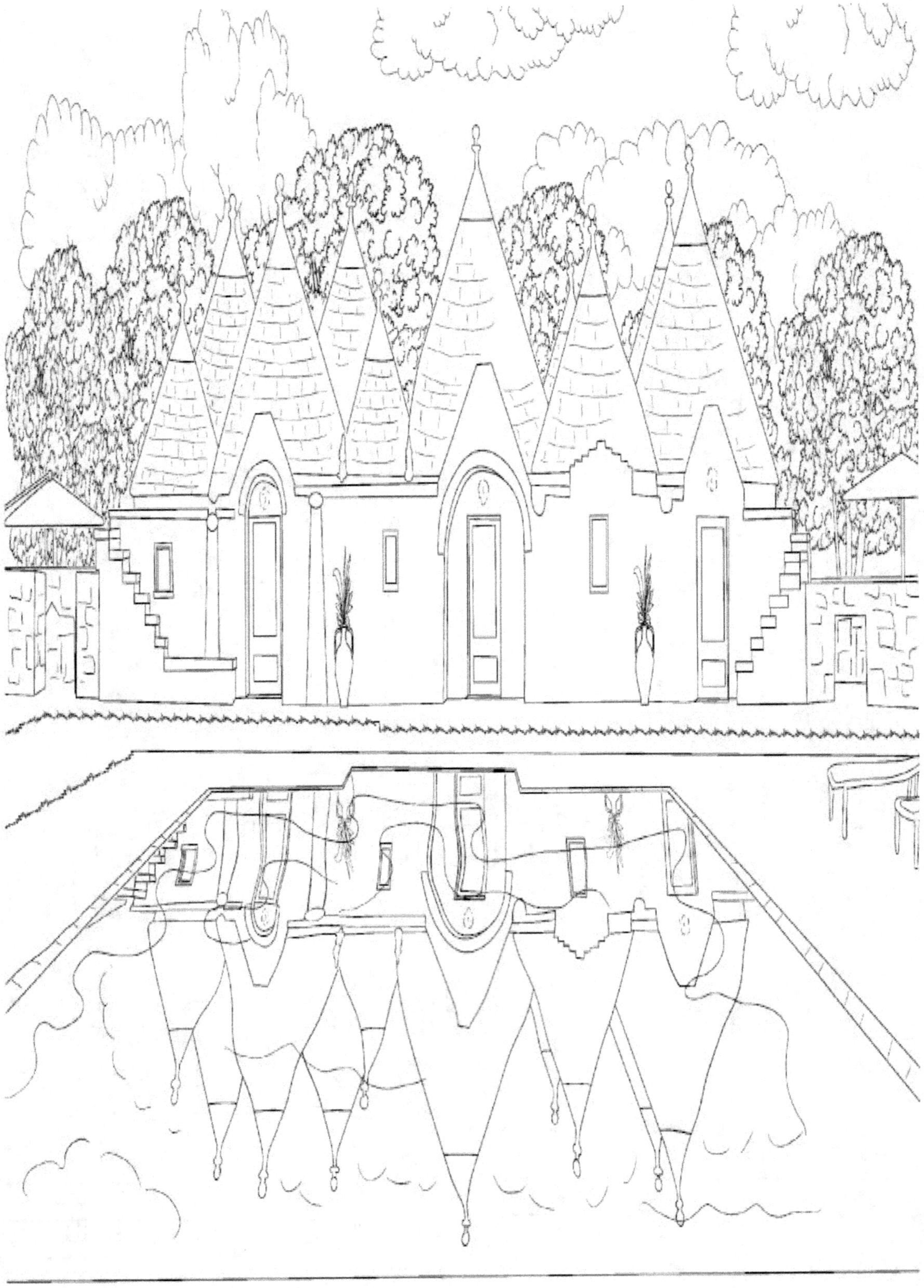

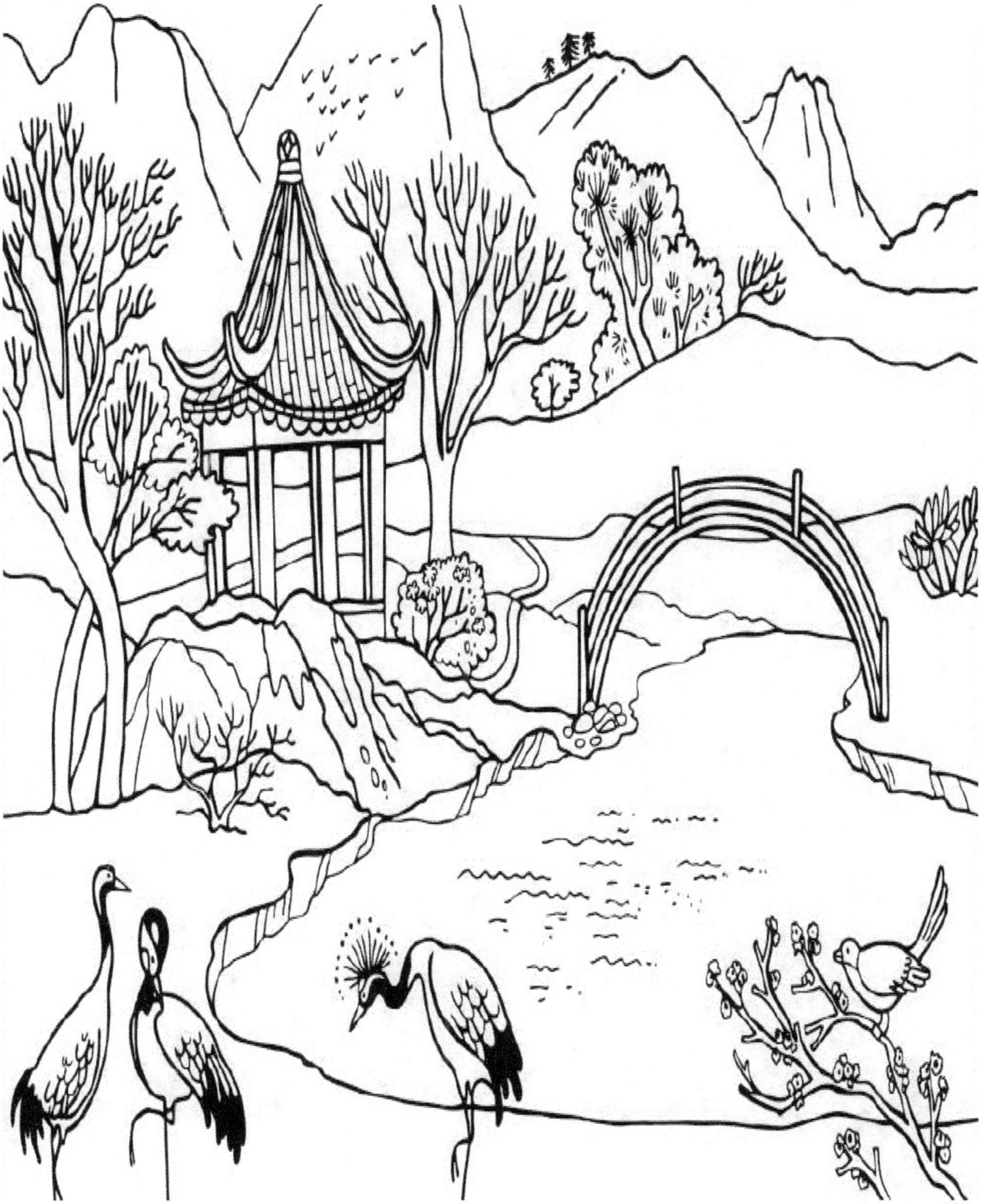

www.ingramcontent.com/pod-product-compliance
Lightning Source LLC
Chambersburg PA
CBHW080617220526
45466CB00010B/3362
* 9 7 9 8 5 7 1 6 8 4 6 2 0 *